MW01519106

1

Noon Publishing Company
Copyright © 2011

The Muslim Family Guide To Successful Homeschooling

Jamila Alqarnain

Noon Publications, California

I dedicate this book to the two most influential women in my life: my mother, Jaleylah Alqarnain, and my grandmother, Helen Person. I can't possibly thank them enough for all of the love and dedication that they put into my education and training. Above all, I thank and praise God for my family and His innumerable blessings. May Allah accept this small effort as an *Ibadah, Ameen*.

Surely my prayer, my sacrifice, my life and my death are all for Allah, the Lord of the Worlds!

(Quran 6:162)

Contents

Acknowledgements

I would like to express my sincere thanks to the extraordinary people who helped make this endeavor a success.

First and foremost, I praise Allah, the Most Merciful Lord! Only through Him are all things possible. I am most thankful to Him for using me to do His will.

Very special thanks to my mom and grandma for giving me a strong foundation and showing me a lot of love and patience in my adolescent years. You both taught me how to be a loving and dedicated parent and for that I am eternally grateful.

I'd like to thank my editors, Asiila Rasool, Kawther Rahmani, and Ke'lona Hamilton (Hamilton-Williams Consulting) for all of your hard work and commitment to this project, the first of many more to come, *Insha'Allah*. I look forward to working with you all again.

To Nazaahah Amin, my very gifted graphic designer/layout artist: I really appreciate the enthusiasm you demonstrated while helping me with this project. You are truly a joy to work with. Thanks are also due to Nhiani Halim for designing my book cover, and Shaheed Williams (Hamilton-Williams

Consulting), who did the final layout design, giving my book those professional touches that really made it shine.

To my sister, Kareemah Alhark, my uncle, Abu Tarleyb, and my dear friend, Haseenah Nuradeenah: I cannot overstate the value of having you all by my side throughout this project. Your advice and words of encouragement gave me the motivation I needed to keep going.

My sincere gratitude goes to the numerous brothers and sisters who shared their successes and trials by contributing their stories, wisdom, and expertise on homeschooling. Your willingness to impart valuable knowledge has not gone unnoticed. If it were not for all of you, this book would not have been possible. *Jazakallah Khair*!

Last, but certainly not least, I want to send out a very special thanks to my lovely family. Much love to my dearest husband, Saleem Abdul-Raheem, who was incredibly patient and supportive during the many hours I poured into this project. I would also like to thank my deeply cherished children for all of their help, sorely needed comedic relief, and for just being the delightful kids they are.

May this book prove to be a beacon of light in the struggle to raise righteous children. *Ameen.*

Introduction

I clearly remember my first year homeschooling my oldest child. My daughter, *Masha'Allah**, learned very quickly, literally teaching herself to read. Indeed, she was easy to teach. Yet there is so much that I know now that I wish I could have known then.

At the time, I didn't know many other sisters who homeschooled, so I had no mentors. As the years flew by, and our family expanded (to the tune of about one new child every two or three years), teaching became more difficult. There was a slight improvement here and there, but overall, I was not happy with the way things were going. By the time my oldest was a teenager, I realized that I was thoroughly killing her love for learning and that of my other children, as well as my own desire to continue homeschooling.

I finally began to seek advice from other homeschooling parents and this helped me tremendously. As we continued on our path towards seeking more knowledge, things remained difficult, but at the same time, I became more spiritual than ever before. I prayed my way through the ups, downs, frustrations and triumphs, and managed to teach my children the basic "reading, writing and arithmetic" that they needed to learn.

Masha'Allah, in the summer of 2010, Allah blessed me with the idea to write a book about homeschooling. I interviewed as many homeschooling parents as I could find (both in the city where I live and on the internet), and my life dramatically changed.

I would like to thank all of the sisters who shared their techniques and who inspired me to implement them with my own kids. The results were instantaneous: My children became happier and more enthusiastic about learning and I became far less stressed out. I can't express how happy I am for this enlightening experience. My life has been thoroughly enriched by this journey that Allah (SWT) has blessed me to embark upon, *Masha'Allah*. My entire family's lives have changed for the better and continue to improve as I learn new teaching methods and philosophies from the new friends that I have made as a result of writing this book.

Parents are guaranteed to make mistakes, but sometimes mistakes can be beneficial to the learning process. At other times, though, mistakes can and should be avoided. If we seek out and adhere to the advice of others who have gained experience in maneuvering their way through all of the pitfalls of homeschooling their children, then we can prevent most of the problems that may occur when homeschooling our own children. As a wise sheikh once said, "You can learn from instruction or you can learn from experience."

Insha'Allah, I pray the following experiences and tips are as beneficial and life-enriching for your family as they have been for mine. May your personal homeschool odyssey bring you and your children closer to each other, and most importantly, closer to our Most Generous Creator and Owner of All Knowledge.

*There is a glossary of Islamic terms included in the back of the book.

Therefore to Allah is due (all) praise, the Lord of the Heavens and the Lord of the Earth, the Lord of the Worlds.

(Quran 45:36)

Chapter 1: Why We Homeschool

Not everyone homeschools for the same reasons. Many people homeschool their children for religious reasons; because they do not want the secular school system "raising" their children five to eight hours a day, five days a week. Others homeschool because they feel that they can do a better job than the government can, especially given the "dumbing down" of school curriculums, the increasing number of undereducated graduates and the decrease in the quality of education. Sometimes, families homeschool simply because that is what other families in their community are doing. I started out in the latter category.

This is me →

My extended family was already homeschooling and I figured, "Why not? Sounds like a good idea to me." After a short time homeschooling my oldest daughter, I found that I loved teaching and being with my children on a full-time basis. In fact, it has turned out to be a very rewarding experience and I feel truly blessed that Allah (SWT) has made it possible for me to stay home and teach my children.

While the number one reason most of the families I interviewed homeschooled their children was the ability, need, or desire to give their children a good

Islamic education, there were some other reasons as well:

 ℠ Homeschooling allowed us to provide an Islamic learning environment while teaching them about Islam, Islamic History, and Muslims, along with their regular curriculum.

℠ I decided to homeschool my children because I wanted them to grow up with the best Islamic education possible. You just can't get that in a public school.

℠ The Islamic schools in the area lack [educational] quality and charge extremely high tuition. I found that I could provide a sound education at home for a fraction of the cost.

℠ The community I am part of promoted homeschooling. It wasn't what I had originally intended to do, but, *Alhamdulillah*, it made sense. So, I decided to go ahead and homeschool my children and I am glad that I did.

℠ I decided to homeschool my children because I wanted to ensure that my kids were in a safe, loving environment where they had lots of individual attention and could thrive and learn.

ဆ When my children were younger, I was concerned that they would pick up values and mores from other children that I did not want to have in my home. It [homeschooling] was a way for me to maybe control that. I also didn't think at the time that they may have been as adequately educated in the basics as I would like them to be. I felt that I could do a better job.

ဆ I've always had a sense of self-sufficiency. I've always dreamt of homeschooling in the same way as home birthing and home gardening. And the whole concept of un-schooling the kids really attracted me. I read a lot of John Holt's books like, *How Children Learn* and *How Children Fail*.

ဆ I can't remember when or why I decided to homeschool. It was just my radical nature. This society is on a bullet to hell and I refused to voluntarily put my children in an environment that engenders a lot of the immoral, amoral and non-God conscious behavior these days. I really am trying to practice what

Gloom!

Islam preaches. I can't see how one does that by putting their children in public schools. Peer pressure is real and powerful, especially as they get older - ten to eleven years and up.

∾ Having said that, I can see how it is possible to let some late high school-aged children (eleventh and twelfth grade) attend public school IF they have proved to be fully committed to the *Deen* and are leaders; they should be able and willing to go out there and influence others vs. being influenced by others. After all, they will soon graduate into the 'real world' and/or college anyway, and must make their own personal commitment to the *Deen*, being able to stand their own ground in their religious and moral convictions. Getting their feet wet at this crucial time - while they're still at home - makes the transition smooth, and can give them confidence in dealing with the outside world and 'others' as unapologetic, upright, Muslim adults. They may even convert some of their classmates! Make sure they attend school with at least one other Muslim child of like mind and purpose.

ಐ I would normally not have known anything about homeschooling, but when I came into the religion it was during a time when the revolution was happening in the United States. Folks were trying to change. They recognized that this nation had a lot of potential, but it definitely needed to change. One of the big elements of change was the civil rights movement and Elijah Muhammad's Lost-Found Nation of Islam. One of the most interesting things about the Lost-Found Nation of Islam was their homeschool program. I believe that they were the first homeschoolers in America. The reason they wanted to homeschool was something that I found really important; they recognized that the system was corrupt. They didn't want their kids to be indoctrinated instead of educated.

We wanted our children to be educated to learn and not just learn how to take tests. Most schools basically teach you how to take tests and regurgitate what is said with no thought of your own. Plus, folks started to dumb down what they taught! We saw that Sister Clara Muhammad and the Hon. Elijah Muhammad didn't send their kids anywhere. They kept them home, talked to them, and developed a really interesting homeschool system. I never was into the Lost-Found Nation because I don't believe in their ideology. I do, however, believe in a lot of their social methodology; homeschooling is one of them.

One sister shed some light on another reason families choose to homeschool:

     ℰ For children who are different, those who have some type of mental challenge or other issue, or for those who learn differently, homeschool is a blessing. As a parent, you can guide their education and can lessen the social stigma that they would experience if they were in a group of ruthless children. This happens too much in our schools, where tolerance is taught less. So, if you don't have a kid that's going in there to be a "star," your kid is going to get trampled on in some way. So many people are homeschooling because they recognize that.

ℰℐ You have young people, who, for various reasons, don't get a good education in the beginning, and never catch up. So, by the time they get to the fifth and sixth grade they're bored, miserable, and want to make everybody else miserable. This makes it harder for your kid to learn. By and large, a teacher can't sit there with a "glock" or an "uzi" and make everybody sit up in their chairs. They can only give the lesson, which is very hard for many teachers because there's such a disparity in skills. There may be a sixth grader who just came here from Africa, sitting next to another sixth grader who just came here from Guatemala, and neither one of them can speak English very well. They're trying, and the teacher is trying to explain the Declaration of Independence when she should actually be explaining to them how to use a can opener. I live in a very multi-cultural area and it is like that. So it's no secret that the public school system has major problems.

You Can Do It!

For those of you considering homeschooling your children, I encourage you to give it a try. I believe that teaching your kids at home is the very best gift you can give to your children and to yourself.

You may feel apprehensive and unsure of yourself. In fact, most of the moms I interviewed felt the same way in the beginning. It's ok! With time you will build confidence, and you will be happy that you made the choice. If you really want to do it, *Insha'Allah*, you can!

Here's some advice from some sisters who have been in your position before:

> ☙ The most important advice that I could offer a family that is considering homeschooling, or someone who would like to but is a little scared, is to just try it! The truth is, even if you fall behind a little bit you can catch up fairly quickly. It really isn't like school where you've got to pull a whole class together with people who are at different levels. If your kids fall behind a little as you're trying to get it all figured out during the transition time, it's ok. It's worth trying because of the benefits. You know, I talk

to kids who were homeschooled and then went back to public school for whatever reason. Oftentimes, it's because the mother felt like she couldn't handle it, she didn't have the resources she needed, etc. But the children still remember their homeschooling experience fondly. I think it's worth it to just try it. Don't worry about things not working out perfectly 'cause they won't. But that's ok too. Public school isn't perfect either, and even Islamic schools have issues. There's good to be found in a variety of situations, but there really isn't anything like having your kids with you.

So I know some parents don't have any other option except public school. I'm not talking about them. But if you have the option to teach your child, you should. I know there are some parents who say, "My kids come home and I can't even get them to do their homework, so how can I teach them?" Homeschool is not like getting kids to do homework after they've been sitting in school all day with some teacher they don't like, and they're dead tired when they come home, and now have to repeat more of what they already did during the day. Homeschool is totally different. You get your child when they are the most fresh, and have them during their best part of the day (when they would normally be at school). It's a whole different family atmosphere.

ജ I can guarantee you that when you start with the right attitude, willing to sweat it out a little bit - because it's not going to be easy in the beginning when you're getting used to it - it will not only get better but it will get easier too. I've heard a lot of people say, "Yeah homeschool, but only if you're patient." They'll talk about me, for example, and say, "Yes, she's really good at homeschooling because she's so patient with her kids, but I don't think I can do it." Believe me, I'm not that patient of a person, may Allah help me. But when I started homeschooling, I read a lot about parenting techniques. I pushed myself and learned to be very patient. I don't have a job where I get paid $10-$15 an hour to problem-solve and learn new skills. I'm at home and I learned new skills and I learned to problem-solve for my own kids and for my family. How can that compare to going and working for a company or even working for the good of humanity or a non-profit?

ℰ It has to be a decision both you and your husband decide to do and you have to be able to put your life on the side for a while to be able to do a good job.

ℰ I recommend "unschooling," along with others of like mind, if at all possible. Utilize the resources in the community. The single most important skill is reading, including retention and critical thinking (logic). The second thing is the ability to research. And not just on the internet. All children should learn how to utilize libraries fully. Also, be willing to accept the different styles of learning and skill and interests that your children have. Not all kids are academicians. Some are better with their hands and they should be allowed and encouraged to become skilled crafts-persons. I recommend reading the section on the necessary crafts of societies in *The Muqaddimah* (a social history) by Ibn Khaldun. Know what their inclinations are - which I strongly reiterate they should be allowed to follow - they all need reading skills and research skills, which will help them all throughout their lives, no matter what they do.

❧ Make sure you are willing to go 100%. It takes A LOT of commitment.

❧ I think that folks really should take the time out to research the history of public schools here in the United States, and they'll see that it was the industrial capitalists that put it into play. They wanted a really educated workforce. I can understand that, but after what happened in the 50s, 60s and early 70s, these people did everything they possibly could to make sure that that sense of revolution and questioning the system would not happen again. As a result of that, if you really want your children to be flexible and have open minds, and really want them to learn for the sake of learning, I think that you should homeschool them.

❧ First of all, I would advise them to talk to lots of families who homeschool.

If they talk to just one family and think, "Oh, I can't do it that way" - independently like I do - they'll be discouraged before they start. Most families are terrified to homeschool that way, but you don't have to file independently in some states.

℘ Find out the different ways to homeschool. There is plenty of support out there. If any part of you feels like you want to, or you could, or you should, or it's better for your family that you do, then take the time to search for options. There are charter schools, online schools, and different support classes throughout the community that can be used to help you along the way. Start with what is easiest, because it's pretty overwhelming at first.

℘ I remember the very first year that I was officially homeschooling. People would ask me, "Are you going to do this till he graduates from high school?" And I was like, "Oh my God, I just want to make it through this year... are you kidding me?" I couldn't think past that. I don't have to do it the same every year. I don't have to worry about next year, since I've got right now. I do that in a context of the goals that we have for educating the kids, but I haven't figured out the practical parts about next year, or two years from now, or five years from now.

Their needs might change by then anyway. If something doesn't work, you can change it. Don't keep going with what's not working. Change it. If you're using this math program and your kids hate it, stop. There are other awesome math programs out there. Also know that what works for one kid might not work for another kid. Even within your own family, things could be different. So my advice is to make lots of *Du'a*, rely on Allah (SWT) since He gave you those kids and the ability to raise them. It doesn't have to be perfect. Regular school is not perfect. People think homeschool has to be as "good" as regular school. But be it Islamic school or public school, it is not perfect. There's still going to be problems. You have to figure out which problems you want to have.

৵ Look at your situation and decide if

you are ready for the commitment. Sometimes it feels like I do nothing but plan and arrange for homeschool! To me, it's worth it. I feel like I have done no greater job on this earth than being a mother and teaching my children. I am attempting to provide the world with some of the best examples of Muslims and I feel that, at this moment, there is no one better suited to bring forth that vision. If this is true for you, I urge you to home educate your children as well.

೮ Prophet Muhammad (PBUH) said it: "Mothers are the first teachers." It's in our nature to teach our children. We can do it. Think you don't know enough? Try writing down everything you know! You'll soon realize you know a LOT.

೮ Teach your children what you know. Chances are, there are skills, wisdom and knowledge you have that regular school never even covers, especially life and spirit skills. Try teaching topics that YOU find interesting. You have hobbies? Teach them to your children. Before public school existed, children learned their parents' skills, as they had to help out (or just watch) at very early ages. Observation, helping and hands-on experience is still the best way to learn. Break it down to your child's level and really get into it. You can teach what you already know or get into something you've always wanted to know. Get excited about it! Think back to when you were a child and there were certain "things" your parents really enjoyed doing and how, almost by osmosis, you began to appreciate them too. Children will definitely pick up on your enthusiasm just because they love you and like seeing you happy and excited to share things with them. And because you feel this way, you will take more time, and find more resources, to also increase your own knowledge base because you like it!

Of course, this doesn't always work. I'm sure you can also remember as a child certain things that excited your parents that did not do a thing for you. Be aware and willing to accept that possibility. Sometimes, you can still teach the subject, maybe change the manner in which you do. Or, sometimes, if it's something they really hate, drop it for a while. My motto is,

"It's better to know than not to know." I can think of at least two things that my parents made me learn that I did not want to learn at the time, but I can now say, *"Masha'Allah,* I'm so glad my parents made me learn such and such."

Stats & Facts on Homeschooling

The Home School Legal Defense Association (HSLDA) released their 2009 Progress Report: *Homeschool Academic Achievement and Demographics,* conducted by Dr. Brian Ray of the National Home Education Research Institute, which surveyed 11,739 homeschooled students for the 2007–08 academic school year.

The results were consistent with previous studies on homeschool academic achievement and showed that homeschoolers, on average, scored 37 percentile points above public school students on standardized achievement tests. The study also found that whether or not parents were teacher-certified had no impact on these high scores. Critics of homeschooling have long insisted that parents who want to teach their own children should become certified teachers first. This study points to the contrary.

(http://www.hslda.org/docs/media/2009/200908100.asp)

"In 2008 more than 2 million U.S. students were homeschooled. This most recent poll, provided by the National Home Education Research Institute (NHERI) proves that since 2003, the number of homeschooled students has more than doubled. The National Household Education Surveys, NHES, says 850,000 students were homeschooled in 2003. In fact, homeschooling is steadily increasing at a rate of 15 percent per year.

"This expansion occurred for multiple reasons. According to the National Center for Education Statistics (NCES), 88 percent of U.S. homeschoolers chose to homeschool because of the public school environment; 83 percent favored homeschooling to provide religious and moral instruction; and 73 percent wished to provide a better quality of academic instruction."

(http://www.sonorannews.com/archives/2010/100707/com mnews_homeschool.html)

There is a plethora of information about homeschooling available online. Do a lot of research. Search your city for homeschool charter schools and public homeschool (independent study) options. Because so many families are choosing to homeschool, many cities offer a homeschool option within the public school system. Find out all of the homeschool laws in your state and compare programs. And don't be afraid to change programs after giving it a decent try. *Insha'Allah,* you will find the right fit for you and your children.

Above all, make lots of *Du'a.* Sincerely ask Allah (SWT) to guide you to the best approach for your family. If you are having a hard time choosing which homeschool path to take, make *Istikharah.* The following *Du'a,* to be prayed in *Sajdah* after *Salah,* is particularly powerful.

When the youths sought refuge in the cave, they said: 'Our Lord! Grant us mercy from Thee, and provide for us a right course in our affairs.'

(Quran 18:10)

Chapter 2: Benefits, Sacrifices and Challenges

Benefits

Aside from the fact that I love having my children at home and forming a strong bond with them while they in turn bond with each other, the biggest benefit of homeschooling is being able to provide a fully Islamic, rather than secular, education. They are inundated with Islamic teachings, etiquette and *Sunnah* behaviors without outside interference. You can't beat the advantages of homeschooling when it comes to your child's spiritual and religious upbringing.

All of the parents I interviewed lit up when speaking about the many rewards they experienced as a result of their decision to teach their children at home.

> ଧ Family time is all day. You have so much more quality time. I feel like I know my boys much better than I would if they were at school. They get to follow their own interests rather than the dictates of a curriculum that wasn't created with them in mind. If we're

interested in something for science, we study it. I don't worry about what is "required" for second graders since grade-based curriculum standards have already decided what that grade must study, regardless of interest.

ℰ Next month we're going to Morocco for *Eid al-Adha* to be with my husband's family. As homeschoolers, we can do this without having to take required work with us, and can use the visit as a form of life experience and hands-on teaching. We'll be learning all about Morocco, its history, its language, and its culture. This is much more educational and real rather than just reading about it.

ℰ When my dad was going to have surgery he needed someone to help him. I have a sister who lives only twenty minutes away from him but she has five kids and they all go to public school and have different bus times. She couldn't go stay with my dad, so I went out of state to be with him. I love the fact that our school is portable. We can go wherever, whenever we need or want to.

 හ We were sending our daughter to the Islamic school, paying a good $400 a month. As you enroll more children, that becomes a hefty price each year. So, one of our homeschool benefits is that we're saving money.

 හ The best thing is that I get to see my children when they're not exhausted after coming home from school. We get to spend lots of time together. I love being with my children. I am thankful for the bond that I have with them and also the bond that they have with each other. I think that they really needed more time with each other and so that's really been a blessing.

 හ It's a chance for me to learn alongside my daughter. We learn so many things together, like the stories of the Prophets. I didn't know much about the Prophets and other such things before teaching my daughter. Homeschooling is an opportunity for us to sit and learn together. I could send my kids to school and have the time to study Islam, but when you're teaching, it's even better. The kids end up reminding you to say the daily *Du'a*, and push each other to memorize Quran.

ھ It's very satisfying when I can look at my daughter and know that she learned this or that from me. It's satisfying knowing that no one loves her like I love her and no one is more invested in her than I am invested in her. I'm going to stand on my head to teach her. I'm going to do whatever it takes to teach her.

ھ Being able to teach my children according to their learning style is a big plus for me. My children are kinesthetic learners, so we do a lot of project-based learning. We have a lot of fun and the children are learning a lot.

ھ I really enjoy teaching my children at home. It's a luxury being able to stay home and do that because it leaves my mind free enough to be totally on them. I can concentrate on them and I don't have to worry and say, "OK, I've got to run to work now."

ھ The first day we start a new task my daughter is shaky. But, the next day I see that she's walking a little taller and going a little stronger. Every bit of progress she makes, makes me feel good about how well I am teaching her, and about how well she is able to grasp the material.

ଈ The pros of homeschooling are that my kids learned to be critical thinkers. At very early ages, they learned how to research their own particular areas of interest and that there are endless resources available to explore them. By not being graded on a bell curve, they learned personal confidence in their abilities and to accept both their weaknesses and strengths. By "unschooling," we had the ability for lengthy travel according to our schedule and opportunities, and they grew and learned enormously from those experiences.

ଈ I like teaching them. I like having them at home helping me cook and they like to help with things around the house. I love teaching my children to read. Reading is one of my favorite things to do, so when they learned how to read and were off reading in a corner with their little books, I felt proud of them and happy that I'd accomplished imparting that knowledge. It's really rewarding that I am the one who taught them all of their phonics sounds and sight words.

ဆ I love the fact that my children learn at their own pace. I have children who learn fast and children who learn slowly. They are able to move along as slowly or quickly as they need to and that is a big plus. If they were in school, they would have to move at the same pace as everyone else and that can be a problem.

Sacrifices

Masha'Allah, the benefits are immense when you homeschool your children. But as with everything in life, there are trade-offs. I had to sacrifice my dream of becoming a fashion designer. At first, I thought that I could juggle sewing, running my household and homeschooling, but instead everything ended up halfway done and we all suffered. My house was a wreck, I was not progressing in my business, and I was not giving teaching my all.

Finally, my uncle sat me down and gave me a good

talking to. "Something's got to give," he said, and I realized he was right. I reluctantly let my childhood dream go. *Alhamdulillah*, looking back, I believe I could have juggled things better if I knew then what I know now. But, I really didn't have a firm handle on my business or on homeschooling, and my organizational skills were nonexistent. At the time, there was no other choice.

I have no regrets. I believe, as many of the other homeschool mothers have said, that all the things you give up mean nothing compared to your child's education and Islamic upbringing.

> ෨ Oh yeah, I definitely sacrificed a career. I wasn't going to be working and homeschooling. It really wasn't that big a deal because I didn't have a whole bunch of career goals when I got married anyway, *Masha'Allah*. I think there were times later on in life where if I didn't homeschool, a career definitely would have been beneficial for me because I had things that I wanted to do. But *Alhamdulillah*, we made those sacrifices for the pleasure of Allah (SWT). I was still able to do some studying and other things I wanted, but definitely not as much as I would have if my children were in school for six

hours a day.

കൻ I would say that I sacrificed quite a bit in order to homeschool. Even to this day I am still sacrificing to homeschool my children. But, *Alhamdulillah*, I believe that, *Insha'Allah*, when they grow up into healthy, religious adults and strong pillars of our society and community, it will be worth it. I think it's already worth it now, and that's why I continue doing it.

കൻ For me, I didn't feel like I sacrificed a career or anything like that. My children were my life, so it wasn't so much a sacrifice as a necessity.

കൻ Yeah, I sacrifice time. It takes up a lot of time. It takes up a lot of energy. I didn't sacrifice a career because I wasn't working. But then again, I don't know if I'd work if I wasn't homeschooling anyway because my husband likes that I stay home.

കൻ I could have a job and be making money while they are at school. I chose to forego that because I can make money later whereas I can't get a second chance to re-do their upbringing. You only get one chance to raise your children.

ﺑ We sacrificed a little in the sense that we are not making $100,000 a year like we could have if everyone was working. But, I feel like, what good is that if everybody is working? There's no spirit in the home; kids are sent off to school and come home drained with a lot of schoolwork; and the parents come home after work tired. Nobody is ready to support each other. What kind of family life is that? So, to say it differently, I don't consider homeschooling a sacrifice, I consider it a gift.

ﺑ I'm still trying to find ways to make sure my needs are met; time alone, time with other adults, so I guess that is my sacrifice. I have less time to focus on my own needs. I also think there is such thing as balance. I just need to find it.

ﺑ I was already at home with two young kids, and was the director of a Muslim non-profit organization. I was very excited about that. That was a big part of who I was and what I did with my life. As I began to homeschool, I really had to spend less of my time focusing on that organization. Slowly, I had to just get other people to step in and start taking over the whole thing altogether. But I probably wouldn't call it a sacrifice because I just felt very strongly that I was making the right decision. I felt that my relationship with my kids and my duty to my family was much more important. So while, in one sense, yes, it might have been a sacrifice; on the other hand, I didn't really feel that way. I just felt like I'm just doing things the way they should be done.

෨ I wasn't employed before so it's not like I'm losing money. Really, the sacrifice in my situation is the freedom to sit on my behind and do as I please like a spoiled queen! Yeah, I'm a little spoiled, but it's my husband's fault. Seriously, since I wasn't working, my sense of usefulness was in teaching my children and giving them the best future possible.

෨ I sacrificed reading time and frivolous off-the-cuff things I wanted to do. Some people say I sacrificed a career, I sacrificed getting a degree, or I didn't get to pursue this and that, but I was able to do that. I already had my degrees; I had already worked (and it's not all it's cracked up to be) before I began homeschooling. I tried working part-time in the first few years of homeschooling, but realized that that was more stress for less money! While homeschooling, I was able to pursue my dream of midwifery because I was able to break away and do that, given the large extended family I have. And because I homeschool, I'm free to change my schedule.

୫ I don't think that I sacrificed that much. Not in the situation that I'm in. In some ways, you do have to sacrifice some things, but instead of looking at it as a sacrifice, I really look at it as a trade-off, or better yet, a trade-up. You have less time for yourself and your house is never clean, but you gain a lot more in return.

Everyone's personality and life situation is different, so you have to evaluate your own situation to determine what you are willing to forsake and what you can pursue in order to have a successful homeschool experience. Figure out what works for you and don't compare yourself to anyone else. You don't have to live up to anyone else's standards and you don't have to prove that you can "do it all." The important thing is that you find you and your family's comfort zone. If you have to stop doing a lot of things in the beginning, don't worry about it. You may be able to pick those things back up later on when you get the hang of homeschooling and as your children get older. Children become less dependent and more independent surprisingly fast.

Challenges

Challenges are an inevitable part of any journey.

Knowing that homeschooling challenges will occur can help you better prepare for them. In fact, you may be able to dodge a few of them altogether. I found that, while every mom and family has some unique issues of their own, there were a few consistent and universal concerns that came up. Some of the ladies laughed jokingly about losing their sanity, which is par for the course in child-rearing anyway. However, I can definitely relate to those sisters who spoke about the financial strain. When I first married, my husband and I really struggled to make ends meet. It was a serious challenge. If I had put the kids in school and gotten a job, we would have been able to live a lot more comfortably, but, *Alhamdulillah*, I refused to give up my goal to homeschool my children. And as Allah (SWT) says in the Quran, "Surely with hardship comes ease." Things got a lot better over the years. I can testify that if you really want something bad enough and pray hard and consistently enough for Allah's help, He will make a way for you. *Masha'Allah!*

ဆ You get a lot of outside pressure. I know I am doing this for the sake of Allah (SWT) and that's what I have to keep reminding myself all the time. The One that I'm going to have to report back to, the One that's going to judge me is Allah (SWT), and not anyone or anything else. I know this, but I still feel like all these people around me are looking at my child and every little problem she has and judging us.

ဆ None of my family members homeschool and none of my husband's family do either. Most of the people we know are not that supportive of it. They look at my child and her progress and judge homeschooling. A lot of people, they have this idea of standards where, by the age of six, she should be able to handwrite this well or be at this level in math, etc. When you are homeschooling, you don't have to follow those standards. One child might start reading early but is not ready for handwriting. There is no reason to sit and force them to handwrite until a little later. But because of the constant scrutiny that I'm under, I always worry if my kids are where they "should be," or wonder if they are missing something that they would have gotten in school. I just feel this extra pressure on me.

೫ It is not easy for me to stay motivated and plan the lessons, either for the month or for the day. I used to be really good at that but for some reason I had a very hard time in this area when I started homeschooling.

೫ I've had some health issues and thus am fatigued a lot. It's a challenge just finding the energy to make sure that we complete the things that we need to complete. After that, the next challenge is making sure that they have a social life. That's one thing that I really feel that they've missed out on and I'm working hard to remedy that.

ఞ Most of the challenges that I face while homeschooling come from me not being organized enough, and the fact that there is no off-day or substitute. So, no matter what I am going through in my life, I still have to teach. I could be tired, sick, having a baby - all challenges. No one's going to come in and do my job for me.

ఞ Having more than one child in homeschool at the same time is a challenge. My children are four distinct individuals with distinct learning styles, distinct strengths and distinct weaknesses. I would say sometimes that is difficult for me.

ఞ I would have to say that juggling was my challenge! Juggling the wash, the dinner, the kids that needed extra help with this and that. Sometimes my husband would bring guests home and I had to cook. The challenging thing was making sure that everyone got what they needed in terms of the amount of time needed to learn a subject while still making it interesting. When we finally got organized and got all the sisters in the community together, it was a little easier because I only had to concentrate on teaching one or two subjects. I was doing Islamic studies and math. Another sister would do science, and someone else would do another subject. When we were all doing it together that made things a lot easier.

 හ My problem is that I'm task-oriented and things have to be done at a certain time. You simply can't do that when you're homeschooling. You have to be flexible, you've got to flow. Because I wasn't that flexible, I found myself getting stressed. And since I wasn't planning the days well either, I found myself always trying to catch up - just being constantly stressed. I have to say overall it wasn't pleasant, but it was worth it.

 හ Kindergarten and first grade were challenging because you have to be there every minute. They are not able to do much independent work so it is a lot more work for you. You have to teach them how to write and all the sounds, over and over, praising and practicing. You can't go over to the next child who is beyond that because the younger ones need you there to show them everything again.

৪০ Homeschooling has actually gotten easier, although I have to say that I had underestimated how much work homeschooling was going to be. I taught elementary school before teaching my own children, but teaching different grade levels at the same time is very challenging. This year, I had a better feel for it and knew the different challenges that I'd be facing. I was prepared mentally and practically, so we're doing a lot better this year. I also had all these ideas about the curriculum that I wanted to use and what we were going to do, but the truth is, I realized that finding the right teaching method is a balance between your personality and your kids' learning styles. So it's taken some time to figure stuff out.

৪০ The most challenging thing about homeschooling I found was the constant pressure of other people interfering and telling me my kids should be in school.

৪০ Now that my son is older, it is difficult to find appropriate activities for his age, especially with Muslims.

ဆာ **Fitting everything in is the hardest thing**. Sometimes when we have a lot to do we just get the basics in. We're doing "classical education" which has a big emphasis on math and reading. So, as long as I get those in first, I don't stress. Math and reading are the most important things.

ဆာ The most challenging situation for me has always been the task of providing enough attention to the younger children while simultaneously teaching the older ones. This is a daily feat and one can never predict the outcome. However, routine is the key.

Whatever challenges you face, it is important to remember that you are not alone in your struggle. Someone has gone through the same issues and can give you some good advice. Join a few homeschool groups, talk to homeschooling sisters you know. Search for online solutions for your specific problem. There is a wealth of information out there and plenty of folks who would love to share their knowledge with you. Again, be steadfast and sincere in your prayers to Allah (SWT) and he will help you through any problems you have. Allah (SWT) answers prayers.

The Holy Quran tells us:

And seek assistance through patience and prayer, and most surely it is a hard thing except for the humble ones.

(Quran 2:45)

Surely I rely on Allah, my Lord and your Lord; there is no living creature but He holds it by its forelock; surely my Lord is on the right path.

(Quran 11:56)

And strive hard in (the way of) Allah, (such) a striving is due to Him; He has chosen you and has not laid upon you any hardship in religion; it is the faith of your father Ibrahim; He named you Muslims before and in this, that the Apostle may be a bearer of witness to you, and you may be bearers of witness to the people; therefore keep up prayer and pay the poor-rate and hold fast by Allah; He is your Guardian; how excellent the Guardian and how excellent the Helper!

(Quran 22:78)

And rely on Allah; and Allah is sufficient for a Protector.

(Quran 33:3)

Allah, there is no god but He; and upon Allah, then,

let the believers rely.

(Quran 64:13)

Has-bi-yal-laa-hu wa ni'-mal wa-keel. Allah (SWT)
is sufficient for me and He is the Best Helper.

Chapter 3: Practical Advice

One of the most exciting things about writing this book is sharing all the valuable tips I received from the many experienced homeschoolers I interviewed, *Alhamdulillah*. This knowledge will help you overcome many obstacles that you may face on your homeschooling journey. This chapter focuses on techniques that will help keep you and your children happy and engaged and the learning environment as stress-free as possible.

The biggest overall advice I have is to make *Du'a*. Make *Du'a* to Allah to help you and believe that Allah will help you. When there comes a time when you just can't see your way, make sincere, specific *Du'a* - Where do I go from here? How do I fix this or that? Be as specific as you can and have faith that your problems will get solved.

Allah has helped me every step of the way. I pray to Him for everything and I see results.

Organization is Key

ℬ If you're not organized in your life, it's not impossible, but it's mighty difficult to homeschool successfully.

ꙮ **You need an area set aside for just-for-school stuff**. You can set it up like a classroom, but the main thing is to have access to all you need where you can go right to it. When you have a home where everybody's coming in and out, they need a place where they can just concentrate on their schoolwork and not be distracted. The kids need an area where they can study, a place where there's not a lot of interruptions and traffic.

ꙮ Calendars, schedules, bulletin boards and to-do lists are my best friends. Put things on your list and schedule, and **be realistic. Don't burn yourself out!** Make sure you put dinner on there. Make sure you have enough time realistically for preparations for dinner. Make sure you have enough time for everything. Write it down. If it looks crazy unrealistic, change it. If you over-schedule, you're going to be stressed out.

ꙮ **Start organizing things before school starts**. Gather together all the things that you need the night before. That way you don't have to run around looking for pencils, paper, books and other supplies.

ॐ **Keep your children's books and papers organized.** Be sure to have them put their books back on the bookshelf or their assigned "home" as soon as they finish with them to avoid a lot of wasted time looking for them later on. Get containers for your pencils, pens, scissors, rulers, erasers, etc. Be sure that all your school supplies "have a home" and they are put back in their home at the end of your school day.

ॐ **Make a schedule and stick to it. If you are finding it hard to stick to, change it.**

ॐ **Read some books on time management and getting organized.** Also read lots of books on homeschooling.

ॐ Lesson plan. Make menus.

ॐ Because I like to have time for myself, I'm a reader and sometimes I'm just in la la land, I learned to stay up after Fajr. Sometimes I was up before Fajr. I traded my time. When everybody else faded back to sleep, I was up working hard. I organized breakfast and might put dinner on. I'd throw in a load of clothes so I'd be finished by 10:00 am. Dinner was pretty much done. I'd have a general idea of what was for lunch and could then sit around and do whatever lessons we were doing. Then out came my book. As long as I kept it like that, I didn't resent what I was doing. I still had time to do what I wanted to do and yet I was able to keep them on a schedule. They were in bed by a decent time so I had my time at the beginning of the day and I had my time at the end of the day. If I wanted to talk to a sister, I would wait until everyone was pretty much winding down around 8:00. I could get on the phone; dinner was already prepared, so when my husband came in everything was set. I had a friend who was always having a fight with her husband, always having problems because she didn't like to get up before 10:00 am, and by the time she got up and finished breakfast and cleaned up, it was time for lunch. She'd be talking to me at 4:00 pm trying to figure out what to make for dinner. I'd ask, "Well, didn't you take something out?" And no, she forgot to take the meat out and the husband was due home in an hour. She stayed stressed out because she spent all day putting out fires because she wasn't organized.

ରେ Oh, I learned to be organized. If you know tomorrow you're going to take the kids to the library, then you take everybody's socks and stick 'em in their shoes before you go to bed. In my house, that was the biggest problem. First, they may not have two socks, and then they might not be clean or didn't match, or wouldn't fit 'cause they couldn't find theirs! That was a big problem before I made that simple adjustment. It made going out in the morning a breeze. Locating a hairbrush, which always seemed to disappear, was another issue. At one time, I kept a hairbrush in my purse.

Keep 'Em Socialized

One of the biggest arguments of those who are against homeschooling is that the children do not have enough social outlets because they are home all the time. While this can be a legitimate concern, it is not a difficult task to overcome. You can make sure your children have a social life with their peers. You just have to be sure to make this a priority.

A lack of socialization can damage your child's view of their homeschool experience. I found that the issue of not having enough socialization came up time and again in my research. It was the number one gripe of most of the homeschooled adults I interviewed. They complained that because they did not have an adequate social life as children, they have poor social skills as adults. The individuals who were able to be around other children were happier being homeschooled. You can avoid this problem if you make sure you arrange for your children to have plenty of social outlets. There are many activities your child can be involved in to give him or her opportunity to learn how to interact with others.

> ε⊃ We had lots of social activities with our family and with the Muslim community. As they got older, they were allowed certain freedoms. I would drop them off at the movies with their friends and pick them back up. They fished, they had a garden. Some of my kids volunteered at the nature center. They would participate in food drives or food give-aways. At one point, we had a food pantry that we created with

another sister and they would help us give out food to certain poor people we knew. We used to collect clothes from the mosque and give the clothes away too.

~ Our kids are taking horseback-riding lessons, gymnastics, art lessons, and they are in weekend Arabic classes.

~ We have play dates with Muslims and non-Muslims. They play soccer, swim, dance, learn Spanish and have a P.E. class. We go to plays and on different field trips.

~ One year we went to a refugee camp to see how refugees live. We learned how to sterilize water and we tasted their rations. That was a great learning experience, *Alhamdulillah.*

~ My children have an air and space class that they take at the museum in the summer time. Also, my oldest son takes a digital media class. My older children take Islamic, math, language arts and mechanics classes with their cousins.

~ My daughter takes a science class with her younger cousins. *Alhamdulillah,* we are blessed to have a nice size *Jamat,* so my kids have plenty of other kids to socialize with.

ఴ We live three doors down from another Muslim homeschooling family, so we have a small network. I also send my children to the local mosque on Sundays to attend the Islamic Studies program, mostly for social interaction.

ఴ I allow my children to have company as much as they like. I have a lot of neighbors that homeschool and we get our children together a lot.

ఴ We had a Muslim Cub Scouts group for a while; that was fun. We have park days and club days with some other Muslim families in the community. They have different sporting activities and swimming lessons. We go on play dates, and we're starting a book club now.

One sister that I spoke with decided that she would organize a group with some of the sisters in her community who were homeschooling so that their children could get together for different activities and socialize together.

෨ That's of course most people's biggest concern - how will your children have friends? That was actually my concern too, so when I started to homeschool that's when I arranged a meeting with the other sisters in my community. I said I'm doing this too, but we'd better all get together and help each other. I wanted my daughter to have classmate-type relationships where she could learn with her peers. We imagined a group of Muslim kids learning together, reinforcing the excitement about being Muslim and learning everything from a foundation of Islam. So we came up with the idea of meeting once a week around planned learning activities. Not with any one curriculum though. We all use different curriculums or are with different charter schools or doing independent schooling, and our kids are all different ages. The idea is to come together and do fun learning, and always tie it back to Islam. So, whatever they're learning, they feel our foundation is Islam. We also get together once a week and go to a park for "play day." *Masha'Allah*, it's a really great group that is growing. On top of that, my daughters are in a homeschool

P.E. class. Every other week we go to a senior citizens home and participate in a gardening club. So, she's with other kids a lot. She's not spending all day in a classroom with other kids her age but she is experiencing people of all different ages. She has much more diverse relationships because of all this. I feel like she has a very healthy social life.

❧ We went to the library and we went to the pier to fish and sometimes we went with other ladies and children to mango groves. We would go to the rainforest, visit the beehives or go to the beach. We had a garden. We lived in a big Islamic community so they had plenty of other children to play with. They were very busy.

It is truly a blessing to be a part of a community where there are a lot of other Muslims homeschooling and who have the same convictions as you. Unfortunately, not everyone lives close to a group like that. If you do not live close to other Muslims, you might consider relocating or simply driving to other sisters' homes for different activities on a weekly, bi-weekly or monthly basis. Find a Masjid where you feel comfortable and attend often so that your children can build relationships.

That being said, do not over-schedule! You have to strike a balance. Yes, we want our children to be well-socialized, but we don't want them involved in so many activities that both you and your children become burnt out. Pick and choose your activities. You can't do everything so you and your kids should pick the ones that are most important to you. And maybe the next year or semester you can try something else on your list. Also, don't compare yourself to others. Sister so-and-so may have her kids in six different classes and seems to have everything going on. That's fine for sister so-and-so. Be happy for her but do what you can do. Do the best you can and your children will appreciate it.

Get Support! Pool Your Resources!

ဆ The best thing to do, I think, is to establish a network of sisters and brothers that have the same commitment to homeschooling. Arrange for all to come together and take part in whatever it is that you all are trying to establish for the children as well as for yourselves.

ဆ   Get   support   from   other

homeschooling Muslims. That's very important because you won't be alone. Whatever issue you're going through, somebody else has already gone through it. It helps to hear that it's normal and learn how they coped. Different ideas work for different kids, so the more people you talk to, the more suggestions you have as an alternative.

෫ *Masha'Allah,* there are so many resources for homeschoolers these days. Be sure that you are utilizing all the resources that are available to you.

෫ One of the benefits that your generation has is that people are forming co-ops now. This is where groups of homeschoolers will come together and teach each other's children. Maybe your child will work with you three days out of the week and then the whole group meets two days out the week. Maybe you're good at math so kids who need help in English go to another sister and kids who need help in math come to you. Or maybe you take them all on an outing. As a homeschooler you can take advantage of that. Let's say you're a mom and you don't know what to do with your fifth grader. You can hook up with some other moms who know what they're doing and then your kid has the advantage of interacting and learning from other adults. You get a break and your child gets help. Sometimes these co-ops will organize sport teams, too.

ಶಿ Check out homeschool blogs and online groups. Check out libraries, thrift stores, and search out other homeschoolers in your community. There are lots of online homeschool sites with tons of helpful information. Google homeschool resources for your city.

All of the sisters I interviewed get some kind of homeschool help from their husbands. Whether he teaches a subject or two, helps with ideas, does hands-on projects with the kids or gives emotional support, all the dads play an active role in their child's or children's education. One thing is for sure, if the husbands do not support the family financially, the role of the "teacher mom" would be impossible, or at least very difficult. All of the sisters I spoke with are very grateful for the love and support they receive from their *Zawj*.

ಶಿ When my husband is here, he helps out with math or whatever I need because sometimes when you have kids that are on three different levels, it helps to have someone come in when they can and help you. No, it's not consistent. He sometimes doesn't have the energy (from working all day) to help, but he's very supportive. Even if the husbands can't physically be there, it's simply the fact that they're the ones bringing in the finances, taking that burden off of us. I don't know if you interviewed any single moms but that would be tough to be responsible for the kids and the finances. That's insanely difficult, I'm sure.

෪ *Alhamdulillah*, my hubby does the Islamic teaching. On his days off, he teaches them how to recite Quran and how to do *Wudhu* and that kind of stuff. He helps me do whatever I need him to do that is easy for him.

෪ My husband is a big supporter of mine, *Alhamdulillah*. I really love the way he supports me. He doesn't really do any of the homeschooling, mind you (laughs), but he'll give me suggestions and reminders to take the children to the park and run them a little while. I counter with, "Why don't YOU take them to the park and run them for a little while?" (laughs) But yeah, he tells me practically every day how great I am and how beautiful he thinks this is, and how happy he is to be able to provide for us so that I can stay at home with the children and homeschool them.

ઠ My husband has always been supportive and active in our children's lives. He is a very practical person who believes in doing something himself before he asks someone else. So, when things broke, the kids helped him fix it. A lot of their interactions with their dad were hands-on. My son learned the metric system helping him change the plugs in his car. The children put the flooring in the kitchen, they figured out how many squares of tile they needed and what they were going to stick it down with. They picked a pattern they liked and they put the tile on the floor. When we were painting our fence, they had to figure out how much paint to buy, how much paint per slat, how many slats, how much a gallon cost, what kind to get, etc. With math, he taught once we got past a certain point.

He also read to them and had discussions. He would try to incorporate some of whatever they were learning into what he was doing with them.

Man Training for Boys

One concern some of the sisters have is their sons picking up feminine habits. This can happen when a male child is around his mother and sisters all day, every day. It is important for boys to be involved with boys their age as well as boys older than them. It is imperative that they have strong Muslim male role models in their life.

   ℬ One of our brothers is a little on the feminine side because he has a lot of sisters and stayed with the girls most of the time. We had to keep reinforcing the idea of manliness and the different roles for men and women that Allah has already defined. To rectify the situation, we had to start asking people to do things with him. For example, if a Muslim brother was doing some kind of yard work, we'd offer to let the boy help. We tried to get him out as much as possible and get other brothers to get him involved in stuff that the men were doing. It helped... *Alhamdulillah.*

෨ We didn't have this issue. The boys were more dominant. They were given responsibilities like leading the *Salah* or calling the *Adthan*. It is important to give them specific duties that are only for brothers.

෨ That was a concern of ours and that's one reason why we started having separate schools. Some families had a lot of girls. My son had two older sisters that were putting bonnets on him and I was like, "No, stop that!" I tried to get them around other boys as much as possible.

෨ We never had that problem. There was a strong male presence in the household. I ran the day-to-day activities, but at the end of the day my husband took charge.

෨ This became a factor at some point and it was because the boys were around girls more. There was really nobody for them to be around so I had to fit them in. I bought Tonka trucks and all kinds of "boy" things while the girls had baby dolls and were learning to cook and whatever. I had one son that didn't want to have anything to do with a Tonka truck; he wanted to play with the doll babies and it became a problem. Although, I didn't see anything wrong with it because boys have to grow up to be fathers too. I thought it was a good education in that sense, but you have to teach the difference between boys and girls and the different roles and skill bases the two sexes have. You have to alert them and let them know that this isn't just a game; this is a process of development. They're learning to be a father figure at some point in time. Really, these issues can come up no matter what situation you put your boys in. There have been situations where boys were kept away and were only with boys, and some other promiscuous things occurred. You just have to do the best you can and make *Du'a*.

Take Care of Yourself

It is very important to get into the habit of taking care of yourself. If you don't, you will get burnt out. It's a guarantee. Worse than that, your physical, mental and emotional health can suffer. Don't overwork yourself and be sure to get away on a regular basis. Go out on dates with your husband and hang out with other sisters at times. Go for a walk by yourself or go have a nice cup of coffee at your favorite coffee shop and bring a book. One sister really summed it up quite nicely:

> ℘ I think the most important thing is, and I would say this to anyone, even if they weren't homeschooling, and to women in particular, since we tend to put others first - TAKE CARE OF YOURSELF!!! I noticed that men usually do not have problems setting their own boundaries and saying no, I need to sleep, or whatever they need to do. Unfortunately, a lot of us women feel that we have to do everything perfectly and we only end up really ruining our health, which makes us no good for those we are trying to care for to begin with! If we're sick and tired all the time, we become moody and end up doing things half way and then feel guilty. Bottom line: investing in yourself is an investment in your family. Be good to you.

Miscellaneous Advice

ℂ **Get a chalkboard** or dry-erase board. Home Depot sells dry-erase boards for a reasonable price. Children love to do their work on the board and I find them to be a wonderful teaching tool. Constantly review past lessons with your children, especially math. A lot of math is revisited every school year, so if you keep their minds refreshed it will be easy for them. If you take a break during the summer, at least have them go through a math review workbook or give them a few problems a day to keep them on their toes.

ℂ Homeschooling is a beautiful thing if you really want to do it, stick to it and try new things. But don't go haywire because there's so much out there and there are so many good techniques. You really have to take a minute, sit back and see what your child's needs are and what feels like a good fit for you to use.

ℂ Don't forget to include lessons on basic life skills. Sometimes we get so bogged down with academics that we forget to include things like sewing, cooking, banking, etc. You don't have to necessarily carve out another hour a day to teach these skills, just remember to have them help or watch you while you do these things. Kids will pick these skills up faster than almost anything.

Insha'Allah, these suggestions will help enhance your homeschool experience. As time goes on, I'm sure you will discover more tips to add to this list. May Allah (SWT) increase your knowledge and make things easy for you as you progress and become "expert homeschoolers."

Inspiring Quranic Ayah & Du'as for Success

Du'a for knowledge:
Rabbi zidnee 'ilmaa.

Translation:
My Lord, increase me in knowledge.

(Quran 20:114)

Du'a for success:
Rabbanaa atinaa fid dunyaa hasanah wa fil akhirati hasanah wa qinaa adhaaban naar.

Translation:
Our Lord! Grant us good in this world and good in the life to come and keep us safe from the torment of the fire.

(Quran 2:201)

When my servants ask thee concerning Me, I am indeed close (to them); I listen to the prayer of every supplicant when he calleth on Me; let them also with a will listen to My call and believe in Me; that they may walk in the right way.

(Quran 2:186)

Chapter 4: Keep It Islamic

Modern Western society promotes secular education and rarely, if ever, mentions God. Religious education is non-existent and very few morals are encouraged. In fact, the bottom-line philosophy of most schools is that morality is "relative." Therefore, the biggest bonus with homeschooling is that your children have the opportunity to be involved with Islam all day, every day. Your child can break for prayer and have Islam integrated into all of their subjects, thus, remembering Allah (SWT) throughout the day. If you teach your children at home, you are better equipped to instill strong Islamic values within them.

We have to understand that our children will not always be with us, and that they will inevitably be under the influence of the society we live in. Our goal is to simply give our children a strong Islamic foundation so that they will be, *Insha'Allah*, strong and committed enough to the *Deen* to resist the temptations of the *Dunya*.

Of course, it is of the utmost importance to keep our household spiritually-balanced or the very influences that we are trying to shelter them from will find their way right into our homes.

     ဢ In some ways it's true, I have not

taught them as much as I thought I would about *Fiqh* and Islamic history, etc. They were getting that in Islamic school and they were getting it pretty well, but there were also other things that they weren't getting that I think they've learned since I started homeschooling them. My daughter decided to wear *Hijab* soon after we started homeschooling, quite out of the blue. I'm not so sure that she would have made that decision if she wasn't homeschooled. I think us having the opportunity to talk and being together a lot more, gave her a firmer grasp on the philosophy behind *Hijab* and other aspects of the religion. We have more detailed discussions than they get in a classroom setting about how to live Islam, what it means to interact with other Muslims, what it means to interact with non-Muslims and so on. I haven't done a great job of giving them the information they were learning in Islamic school, but I think they have learned some really important lessons about what it means to live as a Muslim by being at home with me.

જી You make your own environment. It

can be a hit or miss situation if you mix signals. You can have the Islamic environment, but you can pollute it by allowing all kinds of things to go on inside your home. If you have the opportunity to homeschool the real worth is having the control. Don't allow these crazy TV shows, these video games or whatever in your home! Why homeschool if you're going to let them do all kinds of crazy stuff outside, watch all kinds of crazy shows on TV, get into all this crazy hip-hop that degrades women and all that kind of stuff? If you do, children will come back with all kinds of unbelievable, "crazy," confused and sinful mindsets. Even at home you have to be careful. Don't let them be on the computer all day long just playing around. Imparting Islamic values has to be why you are homeschooling in the first place, you know. It has to be different than going to public school. Why keep the kids out if you're just going to let them run wild at home?

ॐ It is important to practice what you preach. Why is your child going to memorize Quran if they never see you memorize Quran? You should have the

Quran open in front of your child, or at least talk to them about the *Surah* you are studying. I don't do it in front of my children because I can't focus, so we talk about what *Surahs* we're both memorizing. Our children shouldn't think that they are memorizing Quran just because they are kids - no, it is a lifelong commitment to have a relationship with the Holy Quran. Don't expect your child to have a love for the Quran if you don't love it; don't expect them to love the *Rasool* if you never talk about him. You know you have to show them through your own behavior. They get excited about a subject when you are.

෨ Whatever show they watched, I looked right at it with them and I skimmed through the books they got from the library and read the summary on the back cover before they could read it. They used to bring home these big stacks of books and I'd think, "Oh my goodness, so many books!" But still, I had to make sure they were not reading anything that goes against our Islamic morals.

ෆ **Prayer is the most major thing, really.** Allah's name is a constant on our tongues in matters of discipline or reward, in ease or in hardship. Allah's name is often repeated; from the womb to the tomb is what I say. It's supposed to be as natural as eating and sleeping. We also incorporate Quran and *Hadith* into the curriculum. As we move into different subjects, I will bring *Ayahs* pertaining to the subject, especially when doing science. You can do so much with science. It is my favorite subject.

ෆ Keeping an Islamic environment in the home is not just something that I do for the children, it's something I do because I want to live as a Muslim. It's something that I'm going to be held accountable for, so what we have in this home is really a natural result of how my husband and I have decided we want to live our lives. We don't watch commercial television but occasionally we have family movies that I have pre-screened and selected. We don't have a lot of media in our home, magazines or anything like that. We're careful about the kind of media we bring in. We pray our five prayers and the kids pray alone sometimes and sometimes with us. We live an Islamic life. We avoid the *Haram* and enjoin the *Halal*.

I have to say, for us it's been really beneficial to have Muslim family outside our nuclear unit. They're far away and they're not here as much as I would like, but still it's really important for my kids, especially for my oldest daughter, to have a lot of Muslim family - to know that it's not just us living this way. We maintain an Islamic environment, not just in our home but in all aspects of our life. You know, we don't live a different life outside of the home, which I think is really important for the kids to see. When I did my yoga teacher training I didn't take off my *Hijab* once. My kids are a part of everything I do so they go to classes with me and they see that I'm the same person at home as I am when I'm out, no matter who I'm interacting with.

℘ My children basically only watch KPBS when they get to watch television. They are allowed to watch television on Fridays for one hour. We control the content of things that come into our house. I look at their books before they even come out of the library. There are some issues they know not to even bring up. We control what movies they see. Usually, we'll go into the kid section and will pick out a movie or two, but I make sure they're appropriate. When they are at home on the computer, I keep an eye on them. It's important to keep an eye on what they watch. If, in the program or story, there is a lot of deceitfulness, covering up of things and lying to parents, then that's something that immediately gets crossed off the list. There's no way that they're going to watch that and think that that's an acceptable thing to do. Imagine, if they begin to mimic this kind of behavior? What will you do then? It would be your fault as you're the one that let that into your house. They're just children, they're learning from you and you personally have to show them right from wrong. You're not going to show a four-year old some crazy show on MTV and expect that not to affect him. You know it doesn't make any sense. I think that people don't take control over their children in this society and they're always blaming someone else. They have a problem saying this is my fault and a lot of people just want to blame someone else.

෪ It is very important to come to an understanding with your husband early on about what you both do or do not want in the home. I was raised in an Islamic household. My husband was not, so a lot of the things that are innocent to him are not innocent to me. It is a major source of contention between us, but sometimes we can come to an agreement.

෪ People will ask me what I do for Islamic education and how I work that in. For us, that's priority. On days when we're limited on time and we have to sacrifice something, it's not going to be our Quran practice. If we have certain Islamic stories we're going through, or prayers or Arabic lessons, those things are covered first. This is one of the advantages I find in having a private homeschool.

෪ When my oldest son was little, he asked if he could go to *Tarawiyah* prayer so we set a rule that he could go, but he had to pray, not all of it, but some of it; and afterwards he had to sit quietly. We did not want him running and playing, as is the practice of some of the other children. To be honest, we weren't really sure if that was going to work or not but we weren't going to go and just let him run around. So he went, he behaved well and he participated in the prayer, *Alhamdulillah*. He's done that now for four years and of course that means he's tired, but he can sleep in the next day. We just readjust our schedule.

This year, *Alhamdulillah,* he fasted the whole *Ramadan* and went to *Tarawiyah* prayers almost every night. He was able to do that and sleep because we homeschool. My younger son, we actually call him our "*Du'a*-before-we-eat reminder person" because if the rest of us forget, he'll remember and remind us with a "(gasp) Stop, stop, we didn't make *Du'a*, everybody has to make *Du'a*!" *Alhamdulillah*, I am still learning different *Du'as*. As I learn them, I teach them, or I'll see a *Du'a* I'd like to teach them and we'll learn it together.

৯ Every subject we study, we talk about it Islamically. For instance, we just got finished reading "The Farmer Boy" and discussed the dilemmas that came up. We're both reading it together, so we talk about it. There's dialogue that goes on in every subject. If we're reading about the weather patterns, we find verses in the Quran pertaining to weather. And if we're discussing a scientific system, we talk about who made it work like that. You know, it was Allah who invented the system in the first place.

৯ If there are things in the house that the angels despise, you know they offend Allah and the angels won't come in. If you aren't reading Quran in your house, if you're putting questionable things in your house, the *Jinn* and the *Shaytan* can come in. All these things you become very cognizant of because your children spend most of their time in the home. This is their environment and it's not a place to just make sure they have toys to play with. You have to consider what's going to keep the angels around your children, so we prioritize

Quran. The first thing we learn in the morning is Quran and that sets the tone. The most important thing that we will be doing today is Quran. Other things come after that. We don't go to a teacher for anything else except a teacher of Quran. That is a big thing.

&0 When I was teaching my children, Islamic Studies was a priority. We got up, did our prayers and then the older girls would begin their work first. They were independent since I had already trained them. Then we would have breakfast and have the opening *Du'a* and *Ayah*. Everyone had a Quran and studied. We had the Arabic alphabet for the people who were just starting. We had an opening circle where everybody had a *Hadith* pertaining to the Quranic *Ayah* that we had memorized.

&0 What we do in the morning is have Quran time where we learn a *Surah*. We have a *Halaqa*, or both, depending on what's happening. But Quran and Islam is number one. I realized that if we don't make this our priority, then the *Shaytan* takes us and we're distracted, and it doesn't get done. So, we've incorporated science and Quran as much as possible. Since I'm a revert, I don't speak or read Arabic. We do what we can, and *Alhamdulillah,* the school we're with never questions our religious studies.

ଊ I keep it real simple and consistent. I think that's what works best for me. And when I say simple, I mean just constantly keeping Allah on our tongues, constantly bringing Him up. If we're doing science and we're looking at the birds, we praise Allah. We say *"Bismillah"* before we start our work every day. On certain holidays and certain occasions we do a little bit more. We sing His praises constantly and we keep Islam rolling during school because we also keep it rolling all day in our lives. Prayer time is a reminder for each other that it's time to pray, learning certain *Du'as* for that day and things like that also expand our knowledge base.

Integrating Islam Into Your Everyday Subjects

Our lessons don't have to be, and actually should not be, secular. There are many different ways to weave

Islam into every subject. It does take a certain amount of creativity however, but it's not that difficult. *Masha'Allah*, I had the opportunity to interview a sister who explained the entire concept of integrating Islam into your homeschooling really well. She explains how she does it and gives examples:

> ຮ We have done unit studies where my daughter would tell me something she was interested in. It could be insects, mountains or the human body. I would plan the whole month of activities around that. We would talk about what the Quran says about the subject and what is mentioned in *Hadith* scientifically. For example, when we studied mountains, we learned all the mountains that are mentioned in the Quran and the stories of the Prophets. We discussed the *Hadith* that mention mountains as well as scientific miracles in the Quran that talk about mountains and we learned how mountains form scientifically. We also did math activities related to mountains. We did everything around mountains so everything was related. She's always very excited about the topics and I would have a list of activities we would do. Every day, we would pick one or

two of those activities and go for it.

Another month we did insects. My daughter loves insects. There are seven types of insects and we got into greater detail about the ones that are mentioned in Quran, like ants and bees. We would also learn the verses where Allah mentions them and why. You might think that's kind of obscure information, but it's not. First, I'm teaching my daughter what Allah (SWT) uses for metaphors and examples - even the mosquito! - to make a point. So she's building a relationship with the Quran based upon her interests. She feels that if she's interested in something, she can look in the Quran and find out about it. She's learning that anything she sees in life is a sign of the creation of Allah (SWT), therefore this is something she should reflect on about Allah (SWT). So, there are the ants in the story about *Nabi* Sulayman and there's the house of the spider (it's not an insect, it's an arachnid), which is similar to the house of the disbeliever. It is very weak and gives no protection. She learns all these parables and it's really teaching her *Aqeedah*. She's building a relationship with the Quran. Then there's some *Hadith* that mention bugs in them and she learns from these *Hadith* the sayings of the Prophet (SAW). When she learns religious lessons that are tied to academic interests, both stick with her better.

With our insect studies, I did a little research and found a Quran contest that was published online. One of the questions for the kids was to find the eight insects that were mentioned in the Quran. They had the answers listed there so I didn't have to look them up. We found so much on the Internet, just from simple web searches, things that have already been prepared by other people. *Alhamdulillah*, I don't have much knowledge but we learn enough about the stories of the Prophet (SAW) from online and book resources. I even ask my husband sometimes. We brainstorm.

One month, we studied farms and gardens. There's a wonderful story in *Suratul Qalam* about gardeners, so we studied that *Surah*. We also studied *Suratul Qaf*. We did all the stories about farms, and *Zakat*, and we talked about how you have to give a bit of your harvest to purify your wealth. In addition to Quran and *Hadith,* we then did the anatomy of the bug, studied what makes it an insect, and went to the zoo. We even went to the Natural History Museum behind the scenes. They have an entomology department there and we saw how entomologists study bugs, how insects benefit humans, and how they are a blessing from Allah. We learned the things ants, butterflies and ladybugs do and how some bugs protect our crops and the soil. So we learned the science of it. Then we tied it all together in a writing assignment, and she wrote a poem about it.

Teaching this way you clearly see how everything is connected. The truth is, we people divide things into subjects. When you learn around a topic, you realize how all these things are tied together. When we studied farms, we covered farms around the world, especially in Muslim areas. We learned how Muslims live in different parts of the world, how people grow and eat different things in different places. This, in turn, connects you to geography! You end up packing all these subjects together and it's much more comprehensive for the child.

ജ Some Muslim parents really don't like teaching their children history because they don't want to teach them about different civilizations, like the Romans. In the beginning I felt the same way about not telling them about the different gods they had, like Mars, Mercury, etc. I felt the same with a lot of the stories in Greek and Roman mythology. Some are disgusting on top of being idol worship. I wasn't sure I wanted to expose them to that perspective. But the truth is the truth... what happened, happened. You can teach these things we find wrong, but make sure we discuss their perspective at the time, and compare it to what we believe.

There was a Prophet that was teaching the truth, that was teaching monotheism to the people, but they disbelieved and ended up doing a lot of evil things. You then tell your children to use their own brains and logic and ask them which path they think is right. This is what the Roman Empire did, these were their values, this is what they were worshipping, and this is what happened. Yes, they were enormous and great, but what happened to destroy their empire? The point is that Prophets were living throughout all these histories. You start out with them, the stories in the Quran, teaching your child so they have the right *Aqeedah*. The timeline throughout history corresponds with the timeline of Allah's Prophets. So, we'll learn all about the Roman Empire, their technology and such and such. They'll know the history because there are lessons in that history. But what are the lessons going to be? Are these going to be the Romans that we all look back on as having the greatest thinkers of all times, or are these the Romans who were destroyed because of their immorality and their disbelief in Allah? There were good things and bad things within that culture too. Basically, you guide your children through this part of their education with a sense of learning from the mistakes that other people have made. History is studied for the lessons that can be learned from it. That's what I focus on with my kids. They will know history, *Insha'Allah*, I hope, better than anyone else, but they will know what they are supposed to learn from it and will be able to analyze the same pattern that is being replayed today.

I can't emphasize it enough. We can lose control of our home environment so much that our children can be just as inundated with *Dunya* ridiculousness as they would be in a public school setting. Most times, it happens right under our noses and we don't realize it until it's too late, or at an age where it takes even more effort to deprogram them. Be very careful about what you allow in your home. *Insha'Allah*, if you make Islam a priority and view your entire curriculum and day-to-day lifestyle through an Islamic lens, you will be able to protect your children from these influences and gain a wonderful spiritual vibe in your home.

Teaching Your Children Quran and Arabic

Some folks are intimidated when it comes to learning how to read and write Arabic and memorize various Surahs. It is not that difficult, especially now that we have so many online resources. I recommend learning as much as possible before you have children or while your children are little. While taking them to Sunday class at the *Masjid* will help them learn, they will learn a lot more if you are their primary Arabic teacher throughout the week. This can definitely be a realistic goal for you. First, find a really good Arabic program that comes with audio so you can study at home. Be sure that the audio is crisp, clear and slow enough for you to follow. Set aside at least 30 minutes or more a day for studying. Remember, consistency is the key. If you only carve out twenty minutes a day, that's fine, just make sure you consistently do those twenty minutes at least five days a week. If you can find a class or a learned sister who is willing to tutor you, take advantage of that. There is a dear sister in our community who tutors me. I go to her when I get stuck on something or when my kids are about to surpass me. I try to stay caught up so that I can continue to help them.

We have a very good technique for learning *Surahs*. First, we look up the meanings of each word. This is very important. Some Muslims choose to only learn the Arabic words by sound, without learning their meanings. It is best to understand the Arabic words that you are saying because we use them in our prayers to communicate with our Lord. How can we call our *Salah* communication with Allah (SWT) if we do not understand the sounds that come out of our mouths?

We learn what each word means and its proper pronunciation. There are tons of sites where you can download *Surahs* in Arabic. Put them on your mp3 player or make a CD via iTunes. You can learn the pronunciation first and then go back and study the meaning of the words, or vice versa. Sometimes it may take a while to get the pronunciation of an *Ayah,* although young children seem especially wired to pick up language quickly. Just keep replaying the *Ayahs* over and over until you get it. It's also a good idea to carry a small notebook with you so you can read over the *Ayahs* you are learning throughout the day. I've done this while standing in lines at the store, post office, or in a doctor's waiting room. If your children are so inclined, you can have contests and prizes, and have them recite to other family members or other Muslims. Praise is a wonderful motivator. Try it. You'll be surprised at how much you and your child can learn with just a little bit of effort!

Suggested Arabic Programs:

- Rosetta Stone
- Iqra Arabic books

Summary:

- Study Quran, Arabic, etc., first thing in the morning before all other subjects.
- Play Quran and Islamic *Nasheeds.*
- If you have to sacrifice a class because of less time, don't let it be your Islamic studies.

- Always stop for prayers.
- Always make time for Islamic holidays and activities. Make them a big deal.
- Integrate Islam into all of your subjects.
- Monitor the media in your home and keep un-Islamic media to a minimum.
- Learn Quran right along with your children.
- Have lots of Islamic discussions.
- Don't just read and learn about Islam, LIVE IT!

Whoever recites the Quran well and clearly is equal in rank to the angels who record creation's deeds. These angels are gracious, honorable and of lofty rank. He who finds difficulty in reciting the Quran will obtain a double reward.

(Bukhari, Muslim)

On the Day of Resurrection a crown of such brilliance will be placed on the heads of the parents of one who learnt the Quran and practiced on its laws, that its glitter will outshine the brilliance of the sun which penetrates your houses. What then do you think will be the position of the one who himself learnt the Quran and acted in accordance with it?

(Ahmad, Abu Dawud)

Oh ye who believe! Save yourselves and your families from the fire whose fuel shall be men and stones; over which shall be angels stern and strong, they disobey not God in what He commandeth them, and act (only as they are bidden).

(Quran 66: 6)

Chapter 5: Unit Studies & Multi-Level Teaching

Unit study involves teaching several different subjects centered on one theme. Multi-level teaching means teaching different grade levels at the same time. If you can combine unit studies and multi-level teaching, it's akin to home school heaven! OK, maybe not quite heaven, but it is very lovely indeed.

There are many prepared unit studies available for purchase online. You can also plan them yourself. Some topics are easier than others to work around. I suggest trying a few and you may find that you have a knack for it.

A Key Point Is To Plan Ahead

First, you need to choose a topic. Pick something that your child is interested in. Decide exactly what aspects of the topic you want to teach.

Second, research your topic online and always include Islam in your lesson. Look for particular *Ayahs* of the Quran or *Hadith* that relate to your topic. Use a concordance, or index of the Quran, to find *Ayahs* about your topic. Ideas will pop into your head as you do your research.

Third, write down your ideas and find other activities related to your topic. Don't forget the local library for age-appropriate books on the topic.

Finally, collect all the teaching material and supplies needed and go for it! Below are examples of unit studies I have planned. They should give you an idea of how this technique works. Remember, how much or how little to include is up to you. The more you do, the more time you'll spend on the topic. Follow your children's interests. If they are ready to go onto another topic, don't feel pressured to do everything you planned. You can adapt what you didn't do to the next topic. On the other hand, if your child can't get enough of the topic, keep going with it! Add more activities and study ideas. Ask your children for ideas. If they are that interested in the topic, they will have plenty of them.

There are also many, many related ideas you can glean from topic-related Quranic *Ayahs*.

Topic: Birds

Project: Build a simple birdhouse. These are very easy to make. You can order some cut-out-ready birdhouses with everything you need in one package.

Or buy the wood, screws and tools and make it from scratch. There are free building plans online.

Incorporate Math: If you choose to make your birdhouse from scratch, teach a lesson on measurement. Make up math problems about migration, eggs hatching and chicks flying away and bird house sales. Create word problems with division, subtraction, addition, multiplication, etc.

Incorporate Science: Research the different species of birds that live in your area. Find out what they eat. How do birds' wings give them lift? How are airplanes modeled after birds? Which bird is the fastest bird in the world? Which is the smallest and which is the largest? Are all birds predators? Which only eat insects, which eat plants, which eat other birds? Can all birds fly? Do all birds build nests? Do all birds lay eggs? What type of animals are birds - mammals, reptiles or amphibians? Look at the anatomy of a bird; are the bones hollow? Why? What are talons?

Incorporate Language Arts: Have older children write a research paper on the birds in the area, their favorite bird or anything they want pertaining to the subject. Your younger children can draw pictures instead and dictate a story for you to write for them. Or have them copy a short story about birds, or about their picture, written on a blackboard to practice their letters.

Incorporate Social Studies: Identify some birds that migrate for the winter. Where do they go? Compare and contrast the birds' home base to their migratory destination. How do birds help people (food, pets, hunt, and clothes)? Discuss how Allah says animals have communities like people do. Research how different birds communicate, build houses, and have families.

Relevant Quranic Ayahs:

Now with him there came into the prison two young men. One of them said: 'I see myself (in a dream) pressing wine.' The other one said: 'I see myself (in a dream) carrying bread on my head, and <u>birds</u> are eating, thereof.' 'Tell us,' (they said), 'the truth and meaning thereof: for we see thou art one that doth good (to all).'

(Quran 12: 36)

Behold! Abraham said: 'My Lord! Show me how Thou givest life to the dead.' He said: 'Dost thou not then believe?' He said: 'Yea! but to satisfy my own undertaking.' He said: 'Take four <u>birds</u>; Tame them to turn to thee; put a portion of them on every hill and call to them: They will come to thee (Flying) with speed. Then know that God is Exalted in Power,

Wise.'

(Quran 2: 260)

Do they not see the <u>birds</u> above them with wings outspread and contracting? None holds them aloft except the Most Merciful; Indeed, He is, of all things, Seeing.

(Quran 67: 19)

And sent He down upon them <u>birds</u> in flocks, pelting them with stones of baked clay...

(Quran 105: 3-4)

And there is no animal in the earth, nor a <u>bird</u> that flies on its two wings, but (they are) communities like yourselves.

(Quran 6: 38)

Seest thou not that Allah is He, Whom do glorify all those who are in the heavens and the earth, and the <u>birds</u> with wings outspread? Each one knows its prayer and its glorification. And Allah is Knower of what they do.

(Quran 24: 41)

I have come to you with a sign from your Lord, that I determine for you out of dust the form of a <u>bird</u>, then I breathe into it and it becomes a <u>bird</u> with Allah's permission, and I heal the blind and leprous, and bring the dead to life with Allah's permission; and I inform you of what you should eat and what *you should store in your house. Surely there is a sign in this for you, if you are believers.*

(Quran 3: 48-49)

Young children love Prophet Sulayman and his ability to speak to animals. Don't forget the discussion between him and the Hoopoe, a type of bird in Suratul-Naml, 27: 16-28.

Other *Ayahs* that mention birds are 5:110, 12:41, 16:79, 34:10, 38:19, 56:21 and 67:19.

More activities:

- Build a model bird nest
- Go bird-watching
- Make a bird feeder
- Let the children help you prepare chicken or turkey for dinner.

Topic: Bread

Project: Bake yeast bread to learn how yeast makes bread rise. Grow bread mold to learn how mold develops. Look online or in recipe books to find recipes to make other breads: fermented, non-yeast, etc.

Incorporate Math: Teach fractions and measurement

when you bake the bread. Count how many slices in the loaves of bread you buy. How many servings are in a bag of pita bread? Make a word problem to figure out how many cents per slice it costs. Imagine starting a bread-baking business. Figure out how much it costs to make a loaf of bread and then discuss how much you would charge for each loaf.

Incorporate Science: Yeast and mold are microorganisms. Learn about microorganisms, what they eat, and how they reproduce. Ask and discover if some microorganisms cause disease. Compare and contrast different types of microorganisms.

Blindfold the children and have them taste small pieces of bread with different spreads or foods on them (honey, jelly, butter, margarine, etc.) and have them identify what the spread is and how it tastes (sweet, sour, bitter, pungent, salty, etc.) Discuss the sense of taste. Does it taste different when the nostrils are closed? How do taste and smell work together?

Incorporate Social Studies: Study the history of the discovery of microorganisms. Study the history of plagues and other community health problems with diseases caused by microorganisms; how public policy and clean water (municipal water system/sewage system) help keep diseases at bay, etc.

Study the development of civilizations when mankind went from hunter-gatherer to agricultural farmers and the development of bread making. Discuss how almost every society and culture has their preferred bread: flat, yeast, no-yeast, fermented, etc. What other grains, besides wheat, have been used to make bread?

Incorporate Language Arts: Discuss the quote; "Man does not live by bread alone." What does it mean? Have the children write about it. Younger children can write instructions on how to make bread using transition and order words (first, second, third, fourth, then, next, etc.). Read the classic "The Little Red Hen." Discuss the concepts of cooperation, hard work vs. laziness, and "reaping what you sow." Ask them if they would have given some bread to the other animals? Why or why not? Do they think the Prophet Muhammad (SAW) would have given them bread? (This could also be part of social studies and Islamic studies charity, etc.) Take a field trip to a bakery and have the children write about what they saw and learned.

Relevant Quranic Ayahs

Now with him there came into the prison two young men. One of them said: 'I see myself (in a dream) pressing wine.' The other one said: 'I see myself (in a *dream) carrying <u>bread</u> on my head, and birds are eating, thereof.' 'Tell us,' (they said), 'the truth and meaning thereof: for we see thou art one that doth good (to all).'*

(*Quran 12: 36*)

Topic: Milk

Project: Make ice cream (in a bag or can) and yogurt.

Incorporate Math: It takes a certain amount of hours of incubation at a specific temperature to make yogurt. Have the children figure out what time the yogurt will be ready. Talk about temperature, both Fahrenheit and Celsius. Have children calculate how much yogurt they need to make in order to feed everyone in the family a certain amount.

Incorporate Science: Yogurt is made with live cultures. Study how microorganisms called bacteria turn milk into yogurt. Research the health benefits of yogurt. What is fermentation? Is yogurt the only food that is fermented? You can also discuss sourdough breads.

Discuss solids and liquids and physical and chemical changes that may take place when making yogurt and ice cream. Is making ice cream a physical or chemical change; what about yogurt? After you make ice cream and yogurt, experiment with heat. For instance, room temperature and stove heat. What happens with the ice cream and the yogurt? Experiment with different temperatures and heating times.

What is milk? The Quran says: *"**And verily in cattle (too) will you find an instructive sign. From what is from their bodies, between excretions and blood, We produce, for your drink, milk, pure and agreeable to those who drink it.**" (Quran, 27:66).*

What does *"between excretions and blood"* mean? What other animals make milk? What are these animals called? (mammals). Name at least ten different mammals and what countries they originate from. Study the difference between mammals, reptiles and amphibians. What about the platypus? What kind of animal is it?

Study cows and other bovines.

Discuss the issue and controversy with modern processed milk, such as the treatment of cows and the addition of bovine growth hormones and antibiotics. What health issues have arisen from this? What is powdered milk and condensed milk? How are they made? What are they used for? Cook some recipes that call for powdered or condensed milk. Discover the difference in taste, texture and smell.

Discuss Allah's mercy for mammalian mothers (to include humans), in providing the perfect, healthiest, cleanest (germ-free) food for their babies. Discuss the importance of babies being fed with their mother's milk, with daughters, especially. Research what science has discovered of the miraculous nutritional make-up of breast milk. Discuss the Quranic injunction to nurse for two years.

Incorporate Social Studies: In some Middle Eastern, Eastern and African countries, yogurt is a food staple. Learn about the different varieties of yogurt and their origin. Study the history of yogurt. Some cultures drink a lot of milk; some cultures originally did not drink milk at all. Which cultures did not? (Inuit, most Chinese and Japanese.) What other animals, besides cows, do humans drink milk from?

Incorporate Language Arts: Have the children practice handwriting by copying down different yogurt recipes. Write a paper on one of the aspects of yogurt. Write research papers on some of the topics that they discovered in social studies on what is most interesting to them. Go on a field trip to a milk processing plant or farm (if they can, have them try milking a cow) and write about what they saw and learned. Children can write a story on the topic.

Relevant Quranic Ayahs

Two Surahs are named after creatures who give milk: *Al-Baqarah (The Cow)* and *Al-An'aam*, which is often translated as *The Cattle* but refers to all grazing animals: sheep, goats, etc. Another study topic!

And verily in <u>cattle</u> (too) will ye find an instructive sign. From what is within their bodies between excretions and blood, We produce, for your drink, <u>milk</u>, pure and agreeable to those who drink it.

(Quran 16:66)

And in <u>cattle</u> (too) ye have an instructive example: from within their bodies We produce (<u>milk</u>) for you to drink; there are, in them, (besides), numerous (other) benefits for you; and of their (meat) ye eat...

(Quran 23:21)

Topic: Moon

Project: Make a model of the moon.

Make cutouts of the phases of the moon in white construction paper and glue them in order on black construction paper. Make a moon phases flip book. Use the cream in sandwich cookies to demonstrate the different phases of the moon.

Incorporate Math: What is the distance from the earth to the moon? How many miles, kilometers, yards, feet and inches? As the numbers get larger, learn about scientific notation. Introduce and discuss geometry: circles, circumference and radius.

Incorporate Science: Learn about the phases of the moon, lunar eclipse, and the difference between the lunar and solar calendars. Learn about the moon's effect on ocean tides, animals, plants and people. Does the moon give off light or reflect light?

Look at the other planets in our solar system and their moons. Which planet has the most, which the least? How big are they compared to our moon and how big are they compared to the planet earth?

Discuss the difference between the earth's gravity and the moon's gravity. Watch old videos of the moon walk online and discuss the topic.

Incorporate Social Studies: Study the history of moon travel and the civilizations who worshipped the moon. What legends are there about the moon around the world? What did ancient people think the moon was?

Get into the habit of moon-watching. Learn the Islamic lunar months and search for the *Hilal* each month as well as the full moon. Learn to calculate the days of each month by looking at the phases of the moon. Keep track of the lunar eclipses each year, make sure the children either stay up or get up to watch them.

Incorporate Language Arts: Write a poem, song or story with illustrations. Assign a book about the moon and write a book report. Imagine traveling to the moon and write a story about the experience - be imaginative!

Relevant Quranic Ayahs

When he saw the moon rising in splendor, he said: 'This is my Lord.' But when the <u>moon</u> set, he said: 'Unless my Lord guides me, I shall surely be among those who go astray.'

(Quran 6: 77)

Does the Quran reveal that the moon has reflected light while the sun is a source of light? What does that mean scientifically?

See ye not how Allah has created the seven heavens one above another, and made the <u>moon</u> a light (Noor) in their midst, and made the sun as a lamp (Siraaj)?

(Quran 71:15-16)

Allah is the One Who raised the heavens without any

pillars that you can see, then He firmly established Himself on the throne and He subjected the sun and <u>moon</u> . . .

(Quran 13: 2)

The sun and <u>moon</u> (are subjected) to calculations.

(Quran 55: 5)

Allah appointed the night for rest and the sun and the <u>moon</u> for reckoning.

(Quran 6: 96)

For you Allah subjected the sun and the <u>moon</u>, both diligently pursuing their courses. And for you He subjected the night and the day.

(Quran 14: 33)

And for the <u>moon</u> We have appointed mansions till she returns like an old shriveled palm branch.

(Quran 36: 39)

For you, Allah subjected the night and the day, the sun and the <u>moon</u>; the stars are in subjection to His Command. Verily in this are signs for people who are wise.

(Quran 16: 12)

Allah is the One Who made the sun a shining glory and the <u>moon</u> a light and for her ordained mansions, so that you might know the number of years and the reckoning (of the time). Allah created *this in truth. He explains the signs in detail for people who know."*

(Quran 10: 5)

"Blessed is the One Who placed the constellations in heaven and placed therein a lamp and a <u>moon</u>-giving light."

(Quran 25: 61)

Make Learning Fun

When teaching younger children how to count, use manipulatives like popcorn, raisins, or, rarely, something sweet like chocolate chips. They can eat what they count or "subtract" by eating.

Cooking is the perfect time to teach measurement: use measuring cups and spoons and ask what-if questions about feeding twice as many people, or half the amount, and how to adjust the measurements. Also, don't miss the opportunity to teach fractions when cutting up pizza, pie, or even sandwiches.

Utilize graphs for information that pertains to their life: birthdays, favorite foods, colors or books. If your child is a young entrepreneur, they can make sales graphs. Children can keep track and graph outside temperatures each morning for a week. Experiment with lines, circles, and bar graphs and have them decide which they like best. There's a million different ways and reasons to graph, the point is to have fun and learn!

There are tons of fun learning games. GW and other school-supply stores stock many of them. Thrift stores often have inexpensive educational games. Another way to find deals on games and school supplies is going to used curriculum sales. If you know exactly what you want, check eBay or Amazon.

Take a field trip to the historical sites in your city.

Kids love to play store! This is an excellent way to teach the value of money, adding, and some simple business skills. Buy a play cash register and play money. Find things around the house for merchandise, find a nice place to "set-up shop" and you're ready to go!

Get excited about the books your children read. Make sure you read to them from the time they are babies. Your love of reading will surely rub off.

Do at least one science project a month. If you can do more, that's even better. Science projects can be done with basic household items. Again, there are numerous sources online via books or experiments that are already explained and laid out for you based on subject and age.

Masha'Allah, this is just the tip of the iceberg! There are an incredible number of exciting and motivating ways to enhance your child's learning experiences. Just remember to plan ahead, have fun and most importantly, pray to Allah for guidance and help.

Those who patiently persevere, seeking the countenance of their Lord; Establish regular prayers; spend, out of (the gifts) We have bestowed for their sustenance, secretly and openly; and turn off evil with good: for such there is the final attainment of the (eternal) home, gardens of perpetual bliss: they shall enter there, as well as the righteous among their fathers, their spouses, and their offspring: and angels shall enter unto them from every gate (with the salutation): Peace unto you for that ye persevered in patience! Now how excellent is the final home!

(Quran 13: 22-24)

Chapter 6: Teaching With Toddlers

Teaching while juggling toddlers is an arduous task to say the least. I know firsthand that this can be a major source of aggravation for parents with large families. Toddlers fight over toys, whine for food every two minutes, scream and cry over the least little thing while you look on in horror wondering how you can teach with one, two, or three toddlers running all over the place and causing commotion from the time they wake up until the time they go to bed.

With a little organization and creativity you can have a smoother day, *Insha'Allah*. It won't be perfect, but you will be able to get the job done. This chapter focuses on organizing teaching techniques and fun activities for your toddlers.

ജ If your toddlers or younger children are going to be working on projects, prepare everything the day before.

ജ Keep a few special boxes of toys that only come out for an hour or two a day when you work with older children. If you rotate them so they are not playing with the same box all the time, the toys will feel like something new and exciting every time they play with them.

ℵ Provide a special rug for your child to take a nap on every day at the same time. Even if they don't go to sleep, have them lay on their rug and rest. This may be a good time to do any experiments or projects. Or just get as much work done as you can.

ℵ Give your toddler some "schoolwork" to do, too. I give my two year old an old workbook that we don't use anymore and he loves it. He loves pretending to do work like his big brothers and sisters. This keeps him occupied for at least fifteen minutes.

ℵ Include your toddler as much as possible. There are lots of activities that he or she can do on his or her own, but you should not have them play independently for more than a couple of hours. While the toddlers are doing their own thing, you should work with the older children doing things toddlers can't be involved in.

ℵ Stay calm and don't take things too

seriously. Expect that there will be spills, spills, and more spills. Accidents and interruptions come with the territory so don't overreact when they happen. Take a deep breath and try to stay calm. Your attitude can make the difference between a good day and a bad day.

෪ Let the younger children have their own snack time in a separate area that is still visible to you. That should give you at least fifteen to twenty minutes of quiet time. Let your young children help. They can help fix snacks and lunch, sharpen pencils, erase the board, gather supplies, clean up after projects, etc.

෪ Projects for your toddlers to work on independently:

- Cheerio necklaces
- Knob puzzles
- Play-Doh
- Lacing cards
- Containers and lids
- Small dry erase and chalk boards
- Coloring books
- Blocks

- Puzzles
- Lincoln Logs
- Audio books with headsets
- Educational videos

೮ Organization is a big factor when teaching your children at home. If they are restless, and if they are not in a structured, organized situation, they can lose focus and motivation. It becomes frustrating for everyone. Multi-level teaching helps, but it takes planning. You can sometimes get your older student(s) to assist with teaching the younger students. Try teaching all the same subject by breaking it down to each grade level, i.e. English, history, math, etc.

೮ I'd like to say that it is a Herculean task, to say the least. My advice is to keep striving and seek out all available resources. It can be difficult for parents but it's very conducive to the learning process to keep children away from all the outside distractions that have lured many children away from not only learning academics, but also learning our religion.

ℰ One thing that helped a lot is structure. Create a curriculum that's geared towards everyday Muslim routine and rituals, along with academics. Another thing that helped me was to have the older children pitch in with the younger ones. Educational computer programs helped out quite a bit. You can set them up to deal with any subject matter you want.

ℰ I got up really early. I would stay up after *Fajr.* I would pray, read Quran, try to do a little exercise and then look at the lessons for the day to see what everybody had to do. My older kids were already up since they prayed with me. After that, I'd give them a chance to put up their beds and do all the preliminary stuff you have to do before breakfast. They would wash up and dress. I would insist they get out of their pajamas because that just made them lay around all day. After breakfast, we'd study Quran and *Hadith* and sing Islamic songs. I would get the youngest ones started on something while the older ones would be on their own. For a while I'd work with the younger ones to get them started on a project or concept. When the older ones got stuck they would skip that section and go to the next subject or the next area of study. When I was finished with the younger ones, which doesn't take a lot of time - only two hours, when they'd do what they could in that time - I'd go back over to the older ones and we'd cover what they didn't understand. If there were no problems, I'd give them more work to do, or chores or whatever was next on the agenda. I would alternate the level of difficulty too... a strenuous topic for a half hour followed by something light.

ဢ **Breathe, break and relax**. Allow your child to help you. My son helps clean at the end of the day. Join a homeschooling co-op or group if you can.

ဢ **Make** *Du'a*. **Don't give up**! We all get frustrated and want to give up at times. That's when you need to take a **break**. Perhaps you're in a rut and need to overhaul your whole routine. Do it and don't be afraid if it doesn't work. This is all about what is best for you and your family.

Teaching many children who are on different levels can be a daunting task. Unit studies and multi-level teaching are excellent techniques that will help you accomplish this more easily.

    ≔ My kids are on different levels and I teach them simultaneously. I sit one off to one side, and the others are off to the other side. While one is doing independent work (at this point, namely, handwriting skills), I actively work with the other. I'll spend a half hour with one and a half hour with the other. I let them interrupt me if it is something important, otherwise they must respect each other's time.

    ≔ When teaching multiple levels, the more organized you are, the more success you will have. Get organized with bookshelves, crates, calendars and schedules. Strategize and figure out ways to smooth out the areas in your life that are chaotic. If mornings are an issue, figure out what needs to be done to make your mornings run more smoothly. If you're trying to teach Ahmad math and you can barely hear over the commotion that Fatimah and Muhammad are making in the other room, take time to figure out ways to keep them occupied. If your first plan doesn't work, go back to the drawing board and find another solution. Make *Du'a* and ask for guidance. With the help of Allah, you will successfully solve your problem.

෨ Don't wake up in the morning clueless. If you are teaching different levels or have a toddler running around, you cannot afford to be unorganized. None of the ideas for getting organized will work if you do not plan ahead. Plan your day the night before. Make sure you have all the materials you need for school the next day. Reflect on how your day went in the evening. Think about what worked, what didn't and what you can do differently to improve. Be prepared to improvise on your plan if needed. It is very important to be flexible. When plan A isn't working, it's time to make a plan B.

෨ Be relaxed in your teaching style.

෨ Don't chat on the phone during school hours. Let the answering machine pick it up.

ഔ Train your children to work independently. While you work with the younger children, after a while they should be able to work on their assignments or projects without needing much help from you.

ഔ Let your older kids work in the yard or on the porch if the weather is nice. A change of scenery can be refreshing and it will give you time to work with younger children without disturbing your older ones.

ഔ Utilize supplemental classes, online classes and educational DVDs. "Schoolhouse Rock!" is a classic all time favorite of children!

ഔ Read the book, "A Well-Trained Mind."

ഔ If your schedule is not working, change it. Don't get stuck in a rut. Change it as often as you need to. Life is always changing, especially in a large family. The schedule that worked last month may not work this month.

ഔ Once a month, cook and freeze a lot

of food to cut down on the time needed to prepare meals.

꙳ Don't follow one mental activity with another. For example, if you just finished math, work on something easy like art or simply take a break.

꙳ Let your children help you come up with ideas for learning a subject. They will be more excited about participating - and they come up with good ideas, too.

꙳ Teach your child that they need to be able to play or read by themselves sometimes. They should learn that there will not be someone there to entertain them all the time.

꙳ Do not try to make a carbon copy of "school" at your house. If you try to make your homeschool into a public school, it won't work and you will get burnt out.

꙳ Do not overbook yourself trying to teach or run to 50 million classes every day.

꙳ Train your children to be obedient

and responsible. Set rules that they are expected to follow with definite consequences if they do not.

ꜱ Again, always assess your days. It is easy to slide into a rut of frustration, grumpiness and disorganization, especially if this is an old habit. We all backslide sometimes, and this is when we have to take time to reflect, to realize that we have stalled or gone backwards. We can then change our behavior. As long as Allah allows you to live to see another day, you have a chance to do better than you did the day before. Don't give up, and most of all, pray to your Lord sincerely. He will help you through.

ꜱ If you are not a scheduled person, at least have a simple routine that everyone can follow. For example, every morning your children know they have to take a shower, in some kind of order (maybe youngest to oldest), make up their bed, eat breakfast and brush their teeth. Then you can have a chart listing the classes that you will have that day. It doesn't necessarily have to have the times for each class if that doesn't work for you, but at least you know what comes next.

ഇ If one child gets done with their busy work before you are finished helping or teaching another child, have the other take a break until you get done.

In general, teaching is a fun and joyful task, but it can become a dreadful chore if you have to wake up every morning to stress and chaos. Take charge of your home and children. Don't let your situation get out of control. If it's already out of control, get control back, one small step at a time, one day at a time. Don't try to change everything in one day because it took more than one day to get that way. You will see immediate results with just a little effort.

Quranic Ayahs for Success

Allah! There is no god but He - the Living, the Self-Subsisting, Eternal. No slumber can seize Him, nor sleep. His are all things in the heavens and on earth. Who is there who can intercede in His presence except as He permits? He knows what (appears to His creatures) before or after or behind them. Nor shall they comprehend anything of His knowledge except as He wills. His throne extends over the heavens and the earth, and He feels no fatigue in guarding and preserving them, For He is the Most High. The Supreme (in glory).

(Quran 2: 255)

Our Lord! Let not our hearts deviate from the truth after you have guided us, and bestow upon us mercy from Your grace. Verily You are the Giver of bounties without measure.

(Quran 3: 8)

Say: 'Truly, my prayer and my service of sacrifice, my life and my death, are (all) for God, the Cherisher of the Worlds.'

(Quran 6: 162)

Chapter 7: The Teenage Years

Mention the word "teenager" in a room of adults and you'll get a variety of mostly negative reactions. Most people assume that working with teens will always be a problem. However, the truth is, homeschooling your teenager can be a joy. Teens are usually much easier to teach than younger children. They are familiar with the home routine and have the ability to read, understand and follow instructions. They are capable, literally, of teaching themselves. When teens want to learn a new skill, they focus completely on their objective and are determined to master whatever it is that they want to learn.

As they race towards independence and display many adult capabilities, it takes less time and effort to manage them. Everyday living skills build independence, energy and enthusiasm and fuel self-confidence. Teens have a larger knowledge base than younger children and are capable of abstract and critical thinking. They also seek a personal identity. Homeschool makes this "self-building" easier since there is less interference from extraneous peer pressure and modern public school culture. They have time to find and/or create themselves.

Take advantage of the learning assets of the teenage years:

- Explore their interests
- Allow initiative and networking
- Use self-directed learning
- Negotiate your teen's education
- Help them solidify Islamic values
- Allow them more independence while stressing the reality that we can never truly be independent because we are all completely dependent on Allah

Since actual book learning can be as little as two to three hours a day, the remaining three to four hours can be dedicated to using the community and the world-at-large as an after-school resource. Let you and your teen's sense of discovery soar. I advise utilizing some of the many books on homeschooling teens. One of my favorites is *Homeschooling: The Teen Years; Your Complete Guide to Successfully Homeschooling the 13- to 18-Year Old* by Cafi Cohen.

Starting Points

- Help your teen list his or her current projects and activities. Include the things he or she does when nobody is telling them what to do. Use these activities as avenues to increase their education in various areas or make mastering them part of the curriculum.
- Ask your teen: "What have you always dreamed

of doing but have not been able to do yet?"

- List the tasks and subjects you have taught yourself over the last ten years. How did you learn them? Your teen can be a self-directed learner and do the same as you.
- Read a character-building book in addition to inspiring stories about real people. We have plenty of role models, heroes and "she-roes" in Islamic history. Do in-depth research on these people.
- Make a list of your teen's current independent living skills. What skills do you want to add this year?

On the other hand, the stereotype of the difficult teenager is true for many parents. Your teen may have mood swings, become more rebellious and give you a hard time during their lessons. They may flat out refuse to do the assigned work or do it haphazardly and half-heartedly. They may not know how to come out and say how they feel or they might be afraid to. Maybe they whine for attention or act like they don't hear you. Maybe they want more freedom or responsibilities or maybe they are simply overwhelmed with their workload and changing bodies and emotions. A number of sisters shared their experiences with me on how they managed their rebellious teens.

(**Note: Some of the quotes in this chapter are actually

advice from a sister who has done extensive research on the subject of Muslim teens. They are illustrated in a fictional conversation format to maintain the flow of the text.)

ೋ One of my easiest children turned out to be the hardest one once she became a teenager. She was so rebellious and, oh my goodness, at first we didn't know what to do! We made her work mandatory but kept to the basics. When she expressed being interested in art, we let her do reports on her favorite artist. After a while her attitude improved and the rebelliousness passed, but I advise parents to be patient and pray. Sometimes you don't know what to do and you still have to keep their friendship. When the other kids asked why she wasn't studying, we'd explain that their sister had something she was going to do and they should just continue what they needed to do.

ೋ What it is that they're going through is mental change and they feel that they are on the same level with you. They want to do what you do. They're thinking, "Why do I have to do this since I'm an adult too?" OK, but they still need training that's going to bring them some kind of skills so they can take care of themselves. So while they're going through whatever they are going through, it's easier to just try to be loving and supportive. Tell them, "We love you and we support you, but you need some more skills in order to fully take care of yourself."

ഇ I think it's ok for children who are not really performing with the four main subjects to stop for awhile to pursue their interests and/or lighten the learning load to just one or two subjects at a time. They can get their GED later if need be. Sometimes, the power struggle is so heavy that it's better to table the confrontation because you don't want to fight them all the time. I don't mean to table everything and let them be totally free to do nothing, but sometimes you have to let go of the learning schedule just like you did when they were younger. Not everyone is ready and able to handle a full high school load at once, nor do they need to! However, the one subject/topic not to let go of is Quranic and Islamic studies. This cannot be discarded and sometimes it's all that is needed to get them thinking of the reality of their adulthood and the life they will be leading and will be held accountable for. After a more adult grounding in Islam, they may take off in subjects they used to avoid. It's like Quran opens the mind and makes learning other things so much easier. It changes the motivation. They can also follow their interests outside academia. If your daughter (or son) likes to cook, look into cooking classes at your local community college or adult education center - research what it takes to be a culinary chef. If she likes sewing, research what it takes to be a seamstress. If there is a career they wish to pursue, have them start pursuing it! They will need training in whatever it is they are interested in doing.

I read somewhere that the teen years are like the terrible two's. In essence, both ages are when the child is going through the stages of discovering themselves and finding some independence from their parents who, up to that time, control pretty much everything. The parents should not clamp down too hard on the toddler so that they can prevent really rebellious teenage years. I found this to be true in the case of my two children. Born thirteen years apart, I took no nonsense with the oldest when she was two. I had the energy to match and refused to let her get out of line. Her teen years were awful. It's only by the grace of Allah that she returned to Islam. I also think being homeschooled from grades three until graduation gave her a foundation to return to after years of her going so far off the path. On the other hand, by the time my second daughter was born in my late 30s, I was just too tired. When she turned two, I turned her "no's" into a game and gave her choices in order to avoid arguing. I still worked with her and trained her, but I learned to ignore most tantrums. I dreaded her becoming a teen, but, *Masha'Allah,* it was a totally different experience. She too was homeschooled the same amount of time as her sister, but she didn't give me any sleepless nights or too much attitude. *Alhamdulillah.*

৪৹ My youngest daughter was getting into a lot of trouble at the charter school she attended. She was basically bored. We agreed that the day she turned 16 she would get her State ID and enroll in the community college. We told her if she could take and pass two classes, we would move her on to the next level. She had to take developmental math and did fine. For the second semester, she took a full load and eventually graduated from community college with honors. Then she decided she wanted to go to Georgia State and everybody was shocked. She got accepted and also took some journalism classes at American University. She eventually graduated from Georgia State with a degree in journalism and a minor in African American Studies. She's back in college now pursuing a Master's degree. She never took the SAT's or the GED! The first standardized test she ever took was the GRE so she could get into grad school. What I'm saying is that a lot of the success with homeschool, I believe, is in looking at the bigger picture of education. You have to believe in yourself because a lot of people are going to say you are out of your mind and question what you are doing. They'll complain, loudly, that you're not doing this or that, not realizing that you have access to the same information that is given piecemeal in public school. There are certain basics you can access. For instance, in elementary school, there's something called the Dolch list, which is a list of the basic words every child in elementary school should know. In the library, there are recommended lists of certain books children should read, such as the Newberry Award and Caldecott Award books, for example. As children age, have them read the classics too. Eventually they will run across mention of Shakespearean plays and other iconic literature from Western culture. Some teens can be difficult no matter what you did before they hit that age. Sometimes it's our own fault because we remember them as being so dependent and young and so easily manipulated. Then they change. We have a hard time making the transition in accepting the seemingly sudden surge of hormones, independence and confidence. They're no longer little kids that can be manipulated so easily. They now need to understand and be motivated from within. Finding what interests teens help. They have the energy and really get into what they like. Some teens need responsibility and will respond better to others outside the family unit. There are many homeschool or charter programs that make them accountable to someone other than parents and/or have access to classes that teens can attend. Parents can support them by being involved in the teen's work and supporting their tutors, teachers, and other types of learning programs that you find. Make sure you provide an Islamic structure in the home. This will have a lasting affect outside the home, no matter what age your children are.

℘ I only had girls. When they became teens, they got moody and mouthy, just like I was at that age. I was all geared up for battle, but I realized our relationship didn't have to be like the expected estrangement between a mom and her daughters. I thought about what was most important to me when I was their age-fitting in, feeling pretty and male attention were the top three. Being left alone and having the freedom to think, read, and write was important too. I wanted my mom to interact with me more and my dad to tell me how pretty I was. I wanted hugs and kisses from my parents and I wanted their respect. I was a little frightened of growing up and needed assurance that I wasn't a total flake, dork or dummy. I needed praise, and I needed to express myself. So, I tried to meet those needs in my daughters. I had their father give them more daddy attention. He discussed a lot about the attributes of a good husband and what he envisioned them to be as Muslim women, married women, and fulfilled women. I let them wear their style of clothes within the guidelines of *Hijab*/modesty. I didn't expect them to wear a *Jilbab* or *Abayah* like me, although I bought them some, and let them pick them out. We made it a big deal to wear them on *Eids* and sister outings, etc. Otherwise, it was sewing or buying shirtdresses, long-sleeved shirts that hit at least mid-thigh, loose jeans or sweats. She could wear her wild-colored shoes and matching bag, and loud, wild-colored *Hijab*. As long as it was within our parameters, I let her get as creative as she wanted. I gave them privacy, knocking and asking permission to come in to her room. I did not read their diaries. I let them and their best Muslim girlfriends hang out, often. They slept over at each other houses and went everywhere together. I tried to teach them what I knew, observed and experienced growing up, as well as what I've learned as a grown woman. I listened to their concerns, interjecting what I thought, but I did not argue with them when they denied some of my diagnoses. I felt it was important that they be able to disagree (with respect), even though, eventually, mama wisdom turned out to be the truth. At least they felt I would listen, try to understand and accept that we won't always agree. I hugged and kissed them and did girlie things right along with them. We did a lot of talking about "women" things too. We looked for and found some appropriate female organizations that they got very involved in like Muslim Girl Scouts, book clubs, volunteering, and working for a hair-braiding salon. There were parameters. We made it very clear what they were. I think them knowing that they had so much more freedom to decide within those parameters made things easier.

❧ When my children were younger, we

followed the Montessori method of "child-led" teaching. In one of Dr. Montessori's essays on child development, she said that around the age of 14 or 15, about the tenth grade, academics should not be stressed. If a child insists on pursuing a subject, allow them to do so, but as a rule, don't push math, English, science, social studies or anything you've been studying up until this point. She said this is a natural stage of development where the "brain" literally needs a break from the rigors of academic study while the body adjusts to the surge of hormones.

While reading that, I had an "aha!" moment. I was in tenth grade when I had the hardest time with school. I cut classes, and my grades dropped from A's to C's and D's. And I didn't care. All of my friends felt the same way, and we used to sneak off campus to shop, walk around the city, talk or go to the beach. We just could not get into school! By the beginning of eleventh grade, it all changed. We were ready for school again. We felt more focused. The impending end of high school was one reason, but more importantly, I felt like I was ready for the next academic stage instead of being pushed toward it. My husband said he felt the same way at that age - school was torture for him that year as well as the rest of high school. He said if he could have, he would have loved to have graduated and gone on with his life by 15 or 16. And when you think about it, not too long ago in America, 15 and 16 year olds were responsible for all manner of "adult" tasks. They were expected to be. Many married by that time and many societies still do the same.

ℰ When our children hit 13, we noticed their resentment of academics and lightened the load, concentrating on Islamic studies, math, reading and English. We did more projects and had more discussions of real life issues like dealing with the opposite sex, responsibility, etc. We increased the amount of chores they were responsible for and let them figure out when they would be done based on their own schedules. They also helped plan their curriculum and we followed their lead.

ℰ Sure enough, by 14, all but one, who

waited until he was 15, expressed not wanting to do any schoolwork. And we let them "drop out" during that year. The first child didn't know what to do and took a month or so to think about it, getting used to the idea - but once he did, he did not, contrary to what my parents and most other adults said, lay around all day. He read and read and read. He volunteered with children and the elderly. He learned life skills: driving, shooting, archery, jiu jitsu and anything else that interested him. He tried a couple of business ventures. He napped. He did a lot of thinking and sometimes shared his ruminations with us. We had lively, interesting conversations. It was really an awesome thing to see his mind blossom as he began to put the pieces of all he learned and observed and felt to make sense of the world and himself. He was very happy about not being rushed to "grow up" and ended up maturing much faster! He and his father got closer, and he would sometimes accompany him to work. My husband told me that they had many a discussion on "male topics" that cleared up a lot of misunderstandings that he was too shy to ask me.

One night at dinner (which he had volunteered to cook), he nervously asked us, "How do we know Islam is the right way?" This is a common thought for kids who are born into Islam and live in a non-Muslim country. The teen years are when our young men and women must, to borrow a phrase, "be born again" to Islam. So, we talked about religion and did a lot of comparative research between Islam and Christianity, Buddhism, Judaism, Hinduism, etc. We talked politics and religion, what was currently happening in Muslim countries and to Muslims in non-Muslim countries. We subscribed to TIME and NEWSWEEK and read the daily paper and analyzed what was actually being said. He became interested in finding other sources of information to compare with what was being reported. We visited different houses of worship and he asked questions.

All this resulted in a much more in-depth and focused study of Quran and *Hadith*. When we read *Surahs* and *Ayahs* pertaining to various religious and philosophical points, Allah's words became even more meaningful; memorization became easier because we had a framework to understand the truth of what was revealed. It became "real." We became more conversant about our religion, the whys, the similarities, the differences, the history, Prophet Muhammad (PBUH), the other Prophets, etc. He was able to answer questions from non-Muslim friends, or rebut misinformation he heard on the news, TV or movies. Often the younger children would listen to our discussions and contribute. Their insight was uncanny. The other two children, who looked forward to their year off, already had a list of things to discover about themselves and the world. Of course, it changed often, but that was fine.

๛ *Masha'Allah*, by the next academic year - all of our children were ready to officially pick up the books again. And now they genuinely enjoyed learning. They still do as adults. Don't worry about keeping pace with the system. Homeschooling children can finish their entire twelve-year education in less than ten, in reality. In addition, there are so many high school/community college study programs and online learning programs that your child will "catch up." In fact, they'll more than likely surpass their peers because their enthusiasm and outlook will be that much more positive. He or she won't just be learning facts to regurgitate for tests, but will have a template by which to connect the dots and make sense of it all - see how it does or doesn't apply to his reality.

Anyway, I say all this to encourage homeschool parents to follow the advice of Dr. Montessori and leave off academics during one of the teen years. The child's entire life outlook can be infused with confidence, insight and purpose during this year of "self discovery." The rest of his or her education will be a joy for all involved, *Insha'Allah.*

৯ Having peers to interact with is very important to teenagers. However, be very careful who your teens befriend. This *Insha'Allah,* should have been done throughout their childhood, but it's even more important now. Non-Muslim and Muslim teens are doing all manner of *Haram*. If your child hangs out with them, it is guaranteed they will be corrupted. I don't mean they'll necessarily end up doing the same, but the door of "acceptance" will be opened in their minds. All kinds of doubts and rationalizations of how one can do these things "just a little bit" will come to mind. Eventually, your teen, will be a fully-grown adult. They will do whatever they want, good or bad. We don't want to make *Haram* an attractive choice because we've allowed certain friends influence what they think, do and say at such a critical age. We may be held liable!

  ⅒ Study Quran and *Hadith* on this matter. If your children are clear on the dangers of befriending bad people, *Insha'Allah,* they'll drop them. Unfortunately, there are always the Muslim kids who act one way with fellow Muslims and at the *Masjid* and another way when they are alone with their peers. Adults won't notice them and the children won't tell. We can't be with them all the time, so *Insha'Allah* we can instill the fact that ALLAH is!

ဃ My children and I had some real disagreements over this issue. I absolutely forbade certain friends they thought were "cool" or "not that bad." They just had to be upset with me when I refused any contact. In time, many of these friends got into major trouble and my children later told me they were glad I kept them from being with them. Pray to Allah to provide good Muslim friends for your children and go out of your way to find them. If you have to drive for hours once a month to attend events where your teens can find decent acting friends, so be it. Consider moving. Set up your own "Muslim Teen Club" so your children can be involved with their peers and help other parents whose children are also lonely.

ဃ Allow your children to go to *Masjid*-organized camps. For the most part, the ones we sent our teens to were well-organized and fun, stressing a lot of Islamic-themed teen issues. There were always kids whose parents sent them to the camp as a last ditch effort to straighten them out. My children said they and other practicing teens really felt God's pleasure in trying to help the wayward teens get it together. Another option is meeting religious, practicing Christian and Jewish families who have teens and who share the same basic values that we do. You can have family outings and field trips, letting the teens interact.

ɕ As in all experiences in life, if there is a serious lack of decent friends for your teenager, it's a great opportunity to teach patience and *Du'a*, as well as trusting and relying on Allah for all our needs. With every difficulty comes ease! They must learn that there will be times in life when it is better to go without than to settle for something that can make life worse.

ɕ Get even more serious with your Islamic studies. The temptations and urges and distractions for men and women "cubs" these days are incredibly intense. Stress lowering the gaze and being modest and have open discussions of what can happen (and is happening) when Muslims lose their posture of modesty. Befriend and influence them instead of demanding and scaring them into obedience - although depending on the child and circumstance, a little scare (and tough love) may be warranted. You may have to be really firm with banning certain things the teen wants to try. Again, bring it back to the Quran and *Sunnah.* Teens have to know the philosophy behind the rules. Make Islam real by discussing "what-if" scenarios for societal problems. Change the schedule of your school and wake them up for *Tahajjud* nights on auspicious days, two days a week. Encourage them to pick out a *Du'a* they especially like and recite it after they pray. Put Quran on an iPod and challenge them to memorize the longer *Surahs* in Arabic as well as the English translation. Read *Tafsirs* of the Quran together. I used to give gifts for each *Surah* they memorized - sometimes cash or an outing they'd enjoy. Make sure they see you doing what you tell them. We would recite *Ayat al-Kursi* whenever we left the house or went driving all their lives. The concept of "going with God" becomes clear.

ℴ We took our teens out to see what was going on in the streets - the people on drugs, homeless, drunk. We showed them why they should be grateful to Allah for their blessings. We made them volunteer somewhere on a weekly basis: feeding the homeless at established shelters, passing out blankets or toiletry kits to those living on the street. We used to pack a cooler full of ice and water and drive around giving them to the homeless begging at stoplights. We encourage our teens to be proud (not arrogant) of being Muslim and looking for opportunities to express that. It makes them strong. We taught them how to give *Dawah.* We role-played and took turns pretending to speak to non-Muslims about Islam. We discussed how to start conversations. We practiced what to say for all possible responses they could imagine. We encouraged them to try giving *Dawah* to non-Muslim acquaintances and non-Muslim family members

ℴ I began homeschooling when my children were teens. The public school environment was already overwhelming the Islamic efforts we put into their upbringing, but in high school it became totally out of control. The oldest teen really resented being pulled from school, but the rest seemed a bit relieved. We gave them a month or two to sleep in after *Fajr*, read, relax, and think about what they wanted to study. It was important that we began treating them how we expected them to behave, as young adults. It took another six months or so for them to realize we were serious about them learning at home and to realize actual academics didn't take up nearly as much time as it did in regular school. They got more interested in learning at their own pace by doing projects and using online classes. The education part was easy, but certain behaviors and getting the chores done was a losing battle until we came up with "Behavioral Contracts" after constant reminding, talking, explaining and helping and they kept acting like they didn't understand or straight up refused.

We realized they needed to experience consequences for deliberately not fulfilling their part. They helped word the contracts and sometimes came up with harsher penalties than we originally wanted! The contracts forced us as parents to be very clear on what we expected. We included specific details of the behavior that needed to change and how. In turn, our teens were allowed their input and to negotiate for less chores or different schedules or even different chores. As for behavior (for example: not returning *Salaams*, starting fights, bad manners), it gave us all a chance to be specific and discuss the importance of correcting these things. A couple of times our children got us to understand that a few of the things we expected were unfair and we willingly changed the contract to reflect that. Because they were involved in the contract wording, they soon changed their behavior to reflect what they agreed and signed to do. Eventually, we didn't need contracts. They were able to sit down, like adults, and talk out their problems. Our communication skills became much improved.

৯ *DU'A! DU'A! DU'A!* This is the time to demonstrate the power of prayer and *Du'a*. In addition to advising and training your teen, find *Surahs* and

Du'as that you can recite as a family. Make sure you go over the English and the meaning of what is being said. Make a lesson out of them. Remind them that Allah is there for them all the time, and loves the young believer. Remind them to make *Du'a* and prayer all the time. Talking to God is not just during *Salah*! All electronic gadgets (TV, radios, computers, etc.) were turned off by dinner time before *Maghrib* and the rest of the night was quiet with reading, projects and studying Islam as our main activities.

ﷺ Reading Quran individually and together and having a *Ta'aleem* (the teens got adept at giving them too) on the parts of Quran that we read together was our nighttime routine. This was in the last hour before retiring for the night. Having Quran is the last thing on your conscience before sleep is very beneficial. Everyone likes to see their children read. And homeschoolers tend to read a lot. The key with teens is finding books that are appropriate and do not glorify the very vices that we have taught them to avoid. Unfortunately, most "young adult" readers in the libraries now have homosexuality, a lot of premarital sex, and violence, etc., in them. Scour the Islamic bookstores and online sources Islamic-themed novels. *"The Girl With The Tangerine Scarf," "A Voice"* and *"If I Should Speak"* come to mind. Many stories are about Islamic characters struggling with secular values and situations. There are more and more books being written by Muslim writers. Make sure you read at least some of these books. They are perfect avenues to start discussions on the reality of your teen's world and how they can get through it by following the dictates of Islam. I always encouraged my teens to write and publish their own teen books. Maybe my youngest two will take me up on it. I always made sure my teens read a variety of books too, like novels, biographies and autobiographies, historical and scientific books (especially if they showed an interest during our studies), and scholarly Islamic books.

෨ Kill the TV. Our children did not grow up with one. It's obvious at the end of the day just how much time is wasted and how attitudes are corrupted by the ridiculously stupid shows and commercials they subject us to. There's a reason it's called "programming." When they were young, we watched Sesame Street and Blues Clues, etc., but that gradually tapered off. We eventually sold the TV, so by the time they were teens TV was something that other people did. They saw it only when visiting those people. The computer should also be severely limited. Your teens should not have free access to it. Make sure there are pornography filters on all of them. The pornographers are not playing around and purposely name their sites with innocent sounding, educational names. Many teens, especially males, are not strong enough to turn their heads, much less tell you when a totally naked woman (and worse) pops up on the screen after misspelling National Geographic while researching something. Most often, they will be shocked and excited, repulsed and attracted. The urge to see more of the same is elicited. It happened to one of my sons and he began sneaking to see more and more. Eventually, in guilt, he tearfully confessed to what was going on, *Alhamdulillah,* and has stopped. I'd also advise that whatever you deny your teen, make sure you replace it with something else. Be clear on why you're not allowing whatever it is; give them the Islamic reasoning. If there is no Islamic reason not to, then consider letting them go ahead. All we can do is raise them with the best Islamic and educational foundation we can. We should not try to turn them into versions of ourselves. Our kids do not belong to us and have to live their lives.

୫ Our children turned into creatures we did not recognize. Not only did they have major attitude, they were disrespectful and tested the limits constantly. I understood that much of it was a phase of the age, but it was also a bit frightening. It became increasingly difficult to deal with them without screaming, threatening and punishing. As much as I knew I did not want to put them in public school, I was sorely tempted. I knew it would make them worse, but I was about to turn murderous (I'm only half-way kidding). THANK GOD for the book, Muslim *Teens: Today's Worry, Tomorrow's Hope* by Dr. Ekram & Mohammed R. Beshir (Amana Publications). I would recommend this book to any and all Muslim parents. Although they are speaking of teens that attend regular school, it can be just as effective, if not more so, for the homeschool family. The authors provide details on how to accomplish *Tarbiya*, "the process of developing individuals to exemplify Islamic teachings in their daily life and empowering them to be the best they can be." They reinforced that it must begin early in a child's life (which we thought we did) and went on to explain how to be an approachable friend to the teen and establish a clear vision between the teen and the parents. They shared how to help the teen develop a strong and confident personality and most importantly how to elevate the teen's level of Islamic knowledge to Islamic conviction. *Masha'Allah.* Certainly, it's true that our born Muslim children must make a personal conversion in their hearts as they grow up. We were trying to force our teens to do more and more without that conviction, and it was beginning to turn them away from Islam. This book helped us to reverse that by going over the Islamic guidelines for conflict resolution, using case studies and examples, reciting Quranic *Ayahs* and *Hadith,* and being a pretty thorough source. *Alhamdulillah.*

ಬ Quran 66:6: "O ye who believe! Save yourselves and your families from a Fire whose fuel is Men and Stones, over which are (appointed) angels stern (and) severe, who flinch not (from executing) the Commands they receive from Allah, but do (precisely) what they are commanded." This *Ayah* struck me when I first read it. I have made it my mission statement in child-rearing. It clarified just how important and serious raising children are. I was raised pretty liberal with few if any consequences.

My parents wanted me to be free, but instead I felt frightened and lost. I remember thinking that my parents must not have really cared for me because I was allowed to get away with so much. As much as we can be friends and relatively lenient with our children, we must make Allah, Quran, Sunnah, and Islam our main focus. More than any other time of their lives, when my children became teenagers, this *Ayah* helped me realize that I had to set clear parameters and enforce rules. It's not about loosening up, but tightening up. I realized that the teen years would be the last days I'd have any real influence over them. *Shaytan*, who Allah said is our enemy and must be treated like an enemy, is not playing. Teens are a prime target.

We were very strict with our children. I showed them love, but they were never confused that we were the parents and they were the children. They knew all the *Ayahs* pertaining to the rights of the parents over children and how they treat us. It sounds oppressive and domineering to many, but it's not. We did our best to prevent our children from sinning. We didn't make these guidelines up. God said it! Our children had "selective freedom." We selected what choices they could make, but there were other areas that we did not open up for compromise. Homeschooling made it easier because they were not bombarded with that other hell-bound nonsense. Every family has a different dynamic. Each child is different. All I can advise is that we do not fall victim to the lure of always wanting our children to like us, or to make things too easy for them. We repeatedly reminded them of our duty to save them from the fire, as the above *Ayah* says. I said what I meant and meant what I said. I started when they were young, so by the time they became teens, they knew me. We tried to balance compassion with discipline. I found that my children rose to what I expected of them. One or two of them tried to test the limits, but that was squelched immediately. There were certain things that were simply not tolerated and our teens knew it. We didn't have too many behavioral problems at all.

Islamically, it can be argued that there is no such thing as adolescence. The term teen is based on the number of years they've been alive. Once children begin to physically mature (and sometimes before), they are adults. They are young adults, but adults all the same. The concept of adolescence - a span of time between childhood and adulthood - is a relatively new concept. Generally speaking, so-called "adolescence" lasts from ages 13-19. However, depending on the psychologist or child development "expert," adolescence can range from the "tween" years (10-12) up to 30 - again, depending on how these same people define the word "mature." Many successful Muslim homeschoolers follow the more traditional Islamic viewpoint. Teens are considered adults and are dealt with accordingly. They say it makes a world of difference.

          ℘ My middle daughter did quite well with the Calvert curriculum. She took a few courses at the community college, but wasn't quite sure if that's what she wanted to do. So, I let her do a year in an "unschool" program that had just begun around here. One of the main reasons I did this is because the "unschooling" philosophy is to lightly guide children but follow their interests, which they pursue with hands-on projects. Since they were building the school, one of her jobs was to figure out how to parquet the floor in this particular room. So she had to master the math to figure out the dimensions of the room, how many squares of parquet she needed, how many were in a box and how much a box cost. She then had to do the whole thing, which included going to Home Depot and buying the materials. And she actually laid the floor! Through the "unschool" experience of learning, she didn't feel she needed to graduate. She felt more confident and increased her load at the community college. She graduated with honors and went onto Bowie State College for a degree in computers, again with honors. She worked for the National Oceanographic and Aeronautics Administration (NOAA) until she got married. Now, she's a mom. She and my younger daughter do not have a high school diploma and have never taken the SAT's.

ò I have a strong belief that the great benefit of homeschooling is that you are free to follow the model that the Prophet (SAW) gave us: the 7-7-7 plan. First, you play with a child until they are 7, then you teach him or her until they're 14 and until they're 21, you treat them as a friend. "Teenagism" is something new. People used to get married when they were 14, working and supporting their family by 15 or 16. So called "kids" were leading armies during the Prophet's (SAW) time. Very young people had extreme responsibility. I think this teenage phase was created to space out people for the work force. The studies were lengthened to keep the child away from home. This way, the state's agenda to break away from family and become independent from them was firmly instilled. Instead, I think we should really teach responsibility young and prepare our children for adulthood puberty. A lot of people don't understand that my child is an adult and is ready to start contributing to society and following the commands of Allah. By the time a person reaches 14 or 15 years old, they will have an entirely different view of the world. They will be at a point in their lives where they can contribute to the community. The big problem with teenagers is they feel that they're old enough to have all these privileges but they aren't given any responsibilities. And some of them don't want any responsibilities because they haven't been taught to value or want them. Others want the responsibilities but feel like they're being treated like little kids and fulfill that expectation. There is so much in the *Sunnah* of our religion about maturing and responsibility that we have to take it very seriously and apply these teachings. I heard a very good lecture called, "Children Around the Prophet" about how *Rasulullah* dealt with children. This was a crucial part of my research for homeschooling and whether I was going to do it or not.

There are a billion parenting manuals with all the advice on how to get your child to behave and raise them right, but in the end, Allah (SWT) is our Protector and Guide. The best advice I ever heard for homeschooling parents is to pray *Tahajjud* and make *Du'a*. When you're doing your part and your absolute best, Allah will be the One who's actually taking care of your children, *Masha'Allah*. Just follow the advice Allah gives and do your part.

∞ Let's face it. Teens are young men and women. They are growing adult body parts; hormones made for mating are surging. Whether they express it or not, they think it, feel it, know it deep down to their essence. We know that sex within marriage is an *Ibadah*, but outside of marriage it's a sin. Unfortunately, this society plays around with this natural reality, making something beautiful into something very ugly. We also have to realize that many cultures have been corrupted by the attitudes of their colonizers and slave masters whose church viewed sex as a necessary evil. As parents of teens, you have to accept that your cute, quiet, darling, *Hijab*-wearing 12 or 13 year old daughter is a sexual being who is awakening to her sexual heritage, just like your sons. To be truthful, for many girls the thought of husbands, marriage and babies come even earlier than boys - sometimes as young as 9. It is a powerful urge that the Prophet (SAW) addressed when he said to "marry young" and stay married. Know that it is beautiful and natural, *Alhamdulillah*. Teach them that. From the beginning, we let our children know they could marry young. We told them to let us know when they felt they were ready. Of course, we had to establish and keep open the lines of communication and openness so that they would feel comfortable confiding in and sharing with us all of their lives, so when physical maturity became topical, they would do so. We also understood that if our sons or daughters married early they could live with us until they were ready and could afford to move out on their own.

৪৯ We stressed living the *Sunnah*. When we talked about the sexual rules and *Adabs* (a lot!), it was always in the context of marriage. We kept our eyes open to families in the community with children the same age and talked to them about our philosophy. I have to admit that I was very disappointed that the vast majority of the Muslim families were absolutely adamant about making their children finish college or wait until they (the parents) said it was time. They went on to say that they thought early marriages were not realistic in this day and age. We argued that, on the contrary, it is not only realistic but also more necessary than ever. It is an effort to buck up against this society, which condemns Prophetic advice on how to deal with young life. It's now illegal in most states, even with the parents' permission, to get a marriage license until 18 whereas just a generation ago, young men and women were marrying at 15, 16, sometimes younger. Anyway, it was more than a notion to find like-minded parents. Interestingly, when I talked to their children many said they wanted to marry earlier rather than later. Others didn't want to marry at all or at least until they were in their 30s!

಼ As a family we fasted together 2-3 times a week and encouraged a lot of physical activity for both sons and daughters. We did what helped us keep our sexual urges at bay when we were their age. In addition to academics, we stressed how to be wives and husbands as far as the philosophy and skills (ironing, cooking, cleaning, sewing, money management, work ethics, shopping, meal planning, nutrition, gardening, etc.) that you need and gave them more and more adult responsibilities when they requested it or as we saw they needed a challenge to try. By the way, both our boys and girls were taught the same. In other words, by the time our children were 11, 12 or 13, we really concentrated on adulthood training. They learned adult responsibilities and were respected and treated as adults. Before then, we made it clear they were headed for young adulthood and made it sound exciting, counting off the years when they could do more adult things. We called them young men and women from the age of 12, never referring to them as children or kids. They rose to what was expected of them.

৯ One of our daughters approached us at 13, saying she was ready to get married. I must admit, that was a shock! We didn't balk since we didn't know if she was testing us to see if we really meant what we said or if she was serious. So, we began to look for potential husbands for her while talking about the realities of *Nikah* and husbands and children. We had long talks about what she wanted in a spouse, what was important in a husband, stressing that piety was the most important. She began to understand that 13 was rather young, and more importantly that there were very few young men even ten years her senior who were interested in marrying. To make a long story short, she eventually got married at 16 to a young man who was 20. They lived with us for about two years. They talked and got to know each other for a good two years before marrying while our daughter finished up her studies and took the GED and then some community college courses. They did not want children right away and thus she was almost 22 when she had our first grandchild. Another daughter got married at 18 and a son got married at 17. The rest of our children were in their early 20s when they married.

೮ Teenagers are young adults. We just have to adjust our thinking. Once that's done, it's easier to listen to them and help them find their place in the family as grown-ups. I wish I realized this earlier. I clearly remember the difference between viewing my older two as "pain in the behind" teenage kids, and the later ones as "young adult children." Even when they were getting on my last nerve, I tried to react to them with respect for the vast and incredibly fast changes they were going through in this century of all kinds of confusion. I admitted that to them. My attitude adjustment made all the difference in how they saw themselves and me. It was much easier to delegate responsibility, listen to their opinions, respect what they had to say, understand that they are not me, and will never be me. I learned to take them where they were and did not expect perfection. They were already hard enough on themselves! Encourage excellence and sincerely praise their efforts. When they make mistakes, don't berate them or roll your eyes or make snide remarks. It's very easy to get frustrated with young adults because they are no longer children. We too often expect them to know more than they currently do. There's a learning curve for everything. Basically, treat and react to your teens as you would like to be treated and reacted to, especially when you make a mistake.

ဢ We cooperated with each other, especially with their education. It was no longer just up to me to pick their course of study. I wish I had stressed more Islamic studies, Quranic memorization, etc. when they were younger, but it just took a different focus to get them interested in it as young adults. Death was the perfect "in." It became a common topic of discussion. We read and discussed all the *Ayahs* on death, studied books on the afterlife, etc. If someone they knew or someone their age died, it was the perfect time to remember the fact that we all are headed home to Allah and tomorrow is not guaranteed to anyone, including them. In general, I've found teens to be either fascinated or frightened of death and dying. Instilling a healthy fear of God and the inevitability of dying and getting them to understand that this life is preparation for our next one is key. Don't forget to balance that knowledge with God's love and mercy, and all the help He's given to make heaven attainable: Quran, *Hadith*, two accompanying angels at our sides, conscience, grading on a curve and padding points for the amount of good and extra deeds.

ۇ We found some Muslim mentors who worked in fields our teens were interested in. We also tried starting our own business. Help your teen discover what they'd like to sell or provide as a service and give them permission to "go for it." They will. We let our children make mistakes too. We didn't do anything for them, including applying for the business license, making up receipts, keeping the books, etc. We advised them when we thought we should, but, depending on the child, some didn't want to hear it. We backed off. Of course, if they ever needed help we were there to guide them.

ۇ Making money is important to teenagers. Soon enough, they will be required to get out in the world to do that anyway. However, their love of money must be tempered with the reality of what it actually is and how it can corrupt. We really tried to make sure our teens understood what real richness and worth is. We also tried to make them understand that money can never be the bottom line of decisions or choices we make in life. We talked about the history of money, how it is simply a tool and how too much love for it can corrupt the soul. We talked about interest and credit cards, how one had to be very careful when dealing with modern finance. My husband let them see our income and bills and showed how the majority of our money goes to supporting the home. He really instilled in our sons that their role would be to support their families. And even if their wives worked, her money would be hers. They took part-time jobs, but had to pick those that did not require any compromise of our religious practices, i.e., working in restaurants or stores that sold pork or liquor. They tried building their own businesses. They had always been required to save at least half of whatever they made or were given as gifts, so they had sizeable savings accounts. When they wanted us to buy them a pair of shoes, or clothing they liked but couldn't afford, they had to come up with half the price. Eventually, they were responsible for buying more of what we used to provide (hygiene products, underwear, clothes).

ೋ Our sons were responsible for one or two of the house bills. If, for whatever reason, they couldn't come up with the money, we'd pay it. By that time, they felt it was their duty to help out and felt bad, making sure it wouldn't happen again. Our one daughter received the same education and the chance to try her hand at work and business too. One practice that really helped develop their sense of duty and community was the "house fund." This is where all of us donated money *"Fisabilillah"* and it was put into a common fund that we all could borrow from. We were required to return the amount that we had borrowed within a certain amount of time that was written out in a contract.

ೋ Our most important lesson, one that we began earlier than the teen years, was that all the money and possessions we received were blessings from Allah and actually did not belong to us. We taught them that in order to purify our wealth we had to give some of it away in *Sadaqah*. Every time they made or were given money, they had to give some of it away to needy people. If they bought new clothes, they had to donate the same amount of clothes or shoes they already had.

છ It's not all about fun and keeping teens entertained. It's not what up-and-coming adults should be striving for. When our kids became teens, we tried to teach them to find their purpose in life. It's so easy to get caught up in the *Dunya* but Allah has told us this life is an illusion that will quickly pass. The real reality is the *Akhirah*. We tried to turn all our conversations back to this fact. What is the best thing to do in any situation? It's easy to tell the difference between good and bad, but what about the difference between good and better or better and best? How do we serve Allah for the rest of our lives? We found as they began to come to fuller cognizance of the fact that God is with us at all times, that every minute of our life will be accounted for, it was easier for them to focus on spending their time in less frivolity. One book that we found very instructive and helpful - we disagreed with the author on some points and discussed that with our children - was *"The 7 Habits of Highly*

Effective Teens" by Sean Covey. The writing style was very young adult friendly. The author is religious and kept God in the equation. Each teen had his or her own copy. We read it as a family, going through it slowly. We had them do most of the exercises, but tried not to make it seem like another school assignment. We often did not even read what they wrote. In fact, we had them re-read the book two or three times throughout the years. Some were quicker than others, but eventually, they got into developing the seven habits: Be Proactive, Begin with the End in Mind, Put First Things First, Think Win-Win, and Seek First to Understand and Then to be Understood, Synergize and Sharpen the Saw. I found the book to be helpful for my husband and me too!

৯০ Homeschooled children are generally sheltered and somewhat naive. Ours certainly were. We didn't believe it was necessary to raise them in the harsh "reality" of the world if we could protect from all the negative influences out there. We wanted to do our best to make sure the majority of their early formative years were in an atmosphere that was as well-mannered, clean, loving and Islamic as possible.

ℵ However, as they got closer to becoming young adults, we began to expose them to the world they would soon have to operate in. The reality for our African American, black-skinned, sons was that they would have to deal with overt and covert racism. Being Muslim added to their "otherness" too. We discussed how the *Sahaba* and Prophets and others in Islam were treated far worse. We reminded them that Allah put them in an American city in the 21st century, post-9/11. They, therefore, were also granted the ability to strive and thrive during this time. We tried to instill confidence. We got them involved in boxing and other self-defense classes. They got state identification cards by the time they were 11, which is the average age policemen begin to suspect black boys of being up to no good.

ℵ In our neighborhood it was routine for police to stop, handcuff and "run" an ID looking for an outstanding warrant. If there was no ID, it was possible the person would be taken downtown and thrown into a cell until he could be identified. We taught them how to act if stopped by a cop or by gang bangers who tried to intimidate them. We reminded them of *Dhikr* and wearing a *Kufi*. Up until recently, being Muslim in our neighborhood was respected. We had to teach them how to act in stores and in public because of what store owners and other people would assume about three teenage black boys together. It's unfortunate, but it is how it is.

ഇ No matter where you live, you've got to teach your children how to cope with the increasingly dangerous (physically, emotionally and spiritually) world. Encourage them to develop strong, life-long, "I got your back" friendships with other Muslims and decent non-Muslims. They have to learn to be interdependent with others, yet independent of the popular crowd. The Quran and *Sunnah* have the answers. This is the time to make this clear.

ഇ Most importantly, we taught our children that the only thing to fear is Allah. It's more than a notion and can be a lifelong battle, but it is doable. Make it a common topic of conversation. Have "what if?" talks. Stress the *Hadith* that says, "Fear is the shadow of *Shaytan*." Explain that a shadow is something that is made when the light is blocked. The light is God and *Shaytan's* main goal is to block that light from us. *Shaytan* tries to whisper fear into us and we are instructed not to listen to him. God is All-Powerful, while the *Shaytan*, in reality, has none. We don't die any sooner than Allah wills. The only thing to fear is not having prepared for returning to Him.

℘ I often reminded my teens of the fleeting nature of this life, even though it seems like theirs is just beginning. I told them to go forward and to live hopeful, happy and optimistic lives, but to realize this life is the inferior one. I always stressed that we are journeying back to God with each passing day. And like any trip, we have to take the time to prepare. I used metaphor to explain. What do you do when you're getting ready to travel? You pack your things to bring with you, you call ahead to arrange your accommodations and maybe even send some payment to hold your spot. That's exactly what making prayers, *Dhikr*, extra prayers, charity, fasting, enjoining the right and forbidding the wrong, etc. are all about. Every minute of every day, every activity, and every thought is a chance to send supplies, money and things you need to make your destination a good one. *Masha'Allah.* Now all I say is, "Remember to pack!" at the start of each day. They get it.

ॐ We encourage our teens to be activists and be out there with other activists. It's important for the world to see the charitable side of Islam, especially now with all the anti-Islam/Muslim propaganda. I tell my teens that they are inheriting an extremely exciting, dynamic yet dangerous world with plenty of battles to fight and issues to address: poverty, unjust wars, pollution, genetically modified food, water rights, homelessness, violence, child abuse, to name a few.

We took them to various rallies and anti-war protests after fully discussing and making them aware of the history of the problem and the opposing side's argument. They painted protest signs and chanted with the crowd. They really got into it. One of our sons began a campaign against a local proposition and wrote letters to local newspapers. Our daughter, the writer, loved to send editorials to any and all newspapers and magazines about whatever issue concerned her. She began a blog and wants to build a website. Another daughter organized other young sisters and their mothers to put together homeless kits for people in our neighborhood, and other projects for poor people overseas. During *Ramadan,* we began a "Feed the Hungry" program after *Iftar* and especially during the *Eids. Eid al-Adha* was the biggest effort with many of the homeless shelters looking forward to our "Muslim food." We took the girls with us when we cooked and served food at a woman's shelter. We try to make sure that there is an Islamic booth of some sort at as many fairs and community/city events as we can. It's a lot of work and preparation, but teenagers, once they find a cause to be passionate about, can do most of the legwork. They have that kind of energy.

Activities for Teenagers

- Start an Islamic teen book club. Make sure you have scholarly and Islamic novels on your list.

- Have your teens write and direct a movie or other type of show related to Islam. Post it online.

- Teens can write plays and perform them at their Islamic center or go on tour.

- Teach historical events and character development, etc. through movies.

- Some of the classic movies are great for philosophical lessons. Teach children to find the metaphorical meanings or implied connotations in movies.

- Go on field trips using mass transit. Have the teens plan the trip and map out the route. Bring backpacks and food. Make it a day trip. People watch. Have plenty of discussions about society, motivations, how to be safe, practical things they want to talk about, etc.

- Several *Hadith* recommend teaching children swimming, archery and self-defense. Girls can learn to swim in regular classes before they're 9 years old. Later on you can find all-women swimming pools/classes. Martial arts of any form are important for boys. Girls need to know how to defend themselves too. If possible, teach your teens how to shoot.

- Research how to survive both during and after a natural disaster. Have teens help prepare and stock food and survival backpacks. Practice dry runs. Go camping. Teens can join various community programs. Learn CPR and keep your card updated.

- Volunteer at hospitals, elder care, childcare, homeless shelters.

- Start a business as a family or let the teens begin their own. There are plenty of online business sites like Etsy, Ebay, and Amazon, etc.

- Encourage teens to develop public speaking skills. Clear, concise communication is most important. They can give reports or presentations to the family. Look into joining "Toastmasters," an organization that teaches effective public speaking. Join along with them.

- Write a family book. Each member of the family take turns writing a chapter, continuing and changing the plot as they go.

- Enter writing, science, art and other types of contests. Take apart and re-build an old computer, car, radio, etc.

- The young men should be in charge of calling the *Adthan* and setting up the prayer room for *Fajr* and *Maghrib/Isha*. Pray together as a family, or better yet, with other Muslims in *Jamah*.

Du'as for Pious Children

Rabbi hab li mi na saaliheen.
O my Lord! Grant me righteous (children).

(Quran 37: 100)

Our Lord! Make of us Muslims, bowing to Thy (Will), and of our progeny a people Muslim, bowing to Thy (will); and show us our place for the celebration of (due) rites; and turn unto us (in Mercy); for Thou art the Oft-Returning, Most Merciful.

(Quran 2: 128)

Those who say, 'O our Rabb! Grant us pleasure and satisfaction from our spouses and children (so that they never become a source of regret or distress for us in either world when they follow Islam properly), and make our progeny pious and make us pious enough.

(Quran 25: 74)

Dua for Children to Memorize & Repeat Often

Ya Allah, Ya Rahman, Ya Raheem, Ya Muqallibal Quloob, thabbit qalbi 'ala deenika.

O Allah, O Beneficent, O Merciful, O Converter of Hearts, keep my heart firmly and permanently attached to Your religion.

For a disobedient child, recite the following verse after each prayer. They will, *Insha'Allah,* soon become obedient:

...and set righteousness, for my sake in my progeny. Of course, I repent to You and I am one of those who submit to You."

(Quran 46:15)

Chapter 8: Homeschool vs. Public School

Most parents told me that their children absolutely love homeschooling. Others admitted that, while their children liked homeschooling, they missed their friends in public school. I found that children who are able to socialize with outside children are more content overall.

ఌ You know, a lot of people that I know kind of assume that it must be very difficult to be your child's teacher because they think you have to sit and force them to learn things. They think that way because some children are always complaining about going to school and doing their homework, but I have never had to force my child to do her schoolwork. I just say it's activity time or learning time and she's ready, she's there. She knows that it's going to be exciting and that it's something she wants to know about and she's excited to learn.

ఌ They [my kids] love homeschooling, but they also have said to me that they miss their friends. They are happier academically with homeschooling and they like spending time with me, but they miss other children. We are working on making sure they have more outside activities and more opportunities to meet other kids.

ख In the beginning, my son didn't like it much because he missed his friends. He's very sociable. I think he likes homeschooling now. Now he's used to it and he sees the progress that he's made. Now that we go to the homeschooling club, that helps.

ख They definitely love homeschooling and if we do anything that remotely resembles public school, it's just hard for them. They love the experiences they are having at home. They love that they get that time with my family and with my husband's family, so I would say overall they definitely enjoy it. My oldest son has asked for more structure and more classes with kids his age right now, but he doesn't want to go to school. He doesn't want to spend all his time in school and then come home and do homework. He knows his life would be very different.

ଚ I think my children like homeschooling but sometimes they wish they could go to school. I have that more with the older children who would prefer to go out and socialize. My younger children are still pretty enthusiastic about learning. We try to make it so they get to interact with other students and other Muslim cousins and friends. So, *Alhamdulillah,* it's going well with them. The teenagers are having a little bit of a struggle.

ଚ From what I can judge, my children probably did not enjoy it as much as they could have. We had some good days that were fun but normally it was a sigh of relief when we took a day off. If we got behind and didn't plan, then you feel like you have to catch up. And that's not fun at all.

I interviewed some adult Muslims who were raised Muslim and went to public school, others who were homeschooled and some who did both. They told me what they liked and disliked about their experiences.

Homeschool Advantages

ଛ What I remember liking about it was actually spending a lot of time with my parents which I really enjoyed. In addition to my mom, I spent a lot of time with my dad in very informal educational situations. For instance, whenever my dad was outside working on the car, he would get me to help him. I remember that's when I first started learning fractions at a young age because he would tell me to hand him the different socket sizes while he was under the car. He would say hand me a half-inch socket and other such sizes. I also learned the different tools, i.e., a screwdriver, vice grip, etc. There was a lot of this type of informal education. My mother and older sister did the same type of informal math learning when cooking and measuring. We actually enjoyed that a lot. I remember having a lot of free time... my days being free around the house and I think I thrived on that. My parents allowed us to keep a lot of pets and the pets were a part of our homeschooling. They would turn that into an educational thing. I remember enjoying the time I got to spend with them and having a loose schedule.

℘ I liked the fact that I was with family and felt comfortable. It was flexible and Islamic teachings were incorporated into it. Mom did Islamic teachings in the morning after Fajr and we did various subjects throughout the day. The structure was really relaxed, especially for the younger kids.

℘ What I liked about my homeschool education was the fact that I could go as fast as I wanted to. I didn't really want to do it slow because I wanted to get it over and done with. I wanted to go to college and I liked being with my siblings. And we helped each other. I liked that I didn't have to deal with a lot of the peer pressure and things that some of my other friends went through. They went through it and didn't come out for the better. I have to admit, I did want to go and see what it was like going to public school. My older sisters and younger sisters got to go, but there were a couple of us who did not go to the school system at all. We always wondered what it would be like. That's just the nature of things - curiosity. But now that I'm older, I don't think I missed anything because things did not go so well for some of them. I would rather, as an adult, be in the "wondering what I'm missing" category than to have done it and wish to God that I hadn't done that.

ღ I liked homeschool because I was allowed to really explore and increase my intelligence. It seemed I had learned certain things and gained certain abilities sooner than my peers. I never felt like I was behind; I never had any problems as far as what I was learning or how fast I was learning. I've always felt like a smart person and I do attribute that to homeschool.

Homeschool Disadvantages

ღ One of the things that I remember disliking was some of the conflicts that would occur with my sisters. Of course being around the house all the time causes a lot of sibling conflict - fighting over resources that you have to share. I definitely have more positive memories than negative memories so I have a positive view of my homeschooling experience.

❧ Now that I'm looking back on it, I didn't like the fact that we didn't have as much structure. When my mom would get pregnant, school was not continuous. There was no routine, no schedule. We had a lot of breaks. When I went to public school, I realized that I needed more structure.

❧ This may be more of a problem for someone who is an only child, but sometimes isolation can be a problem for large families too. We were isolated because we were in a very, very small town. We did not have buses or taxis to get out and about and it's hard to come up with things to do in a large family. It is harder to do things with children. Mind you, we got a lot of experiences with things that you can do with large families and it was fun, but sometimes we felt a little bit isolated. I think mostly it was because of the place that we lived; there just wasn't a lot to do. What do you do when there are no buses or taxis? Or just one taxi that came basically when he wanted to because he had no competition? There was no mall and there was no movie theater. We did coordinate with other mothers and other homeschoolers and with other Muslims that homeschooled. One time we had a fashion show. There was a basket-weaving class that this woman taught. Each woman had specific skills and they organized so that they could share those skills with us. We did sewing class one time and there was one woman who knew how to knit. There was crocheting, doing hair, and we learned the womanly art of running a home. That is an art that is actually being lost.

ဢ I was less confident around strangers as there were fewer interactions with them. We weren't exposed to a lot of sports and social activities. We didn't get a broader perspective on things and had trouble with social interactions. We spent most of the time being around family and a small number of people in the community.

ဢ As far as socializing, I think my parents were lacking in that. Me and my siblings all came to the consensus that what sucked the most was not having access to friends. We didn't live in a neighborhood with lots of kids and we were on a busy street. It was hard to be able to have constant interaction with other people my age. I had relatives my age but based on the dynamics of my family, we rarely got together. Later on, when I was like 10 or 11, my parents put me in martial arts. That really helped because I was around other kids and socializing with other people my age, which I had never done before. The martial arts classes made me want to know what regular school was like, so I ended up going to a charter school that same year.

Public School Advantages

so When I first went to public school, I don't think I liked it much at all. To be honest, what I remember liking about public school was being smarter than everybody else. At first, I got clowned hard for the first time in my life because I wasn't fashionable. I didn't know anything about fashion then. I had been dressed the whole time by my parents and they weren't judging my fashion as a 9 or 10 year old would. So as soon as I got around my peers, my goodness, I started getting very self-conscious. I wanted to dress nice to look good for the cute young girls in the class. Definitely, being in that co-ed environment at a young age, being thrown into that was a whole other thing I had to deal with, something I didn't have to deal with just being at home. The other thing I liked about public school was that I was able to do well. The teachers liked me. I was a good student. I had a couple of good friends that were all on safety patrol. I thought that was cool. It was a job they gave the kids they felt had a degree of responsibility. So a couple of other kids that I became good friends with were also on safety patrol, helping folks cross the street. Those were a couple of things that I liked, those friends and teachers and being able to do well academically.

&o Oddly enough, the thing I most loved about school was also the thing I most disliked, and that was the social factor. I had some of the best buddies and went to school with some of the most interesting characters from elementary to high school. There were approximately twenty students who accompanied each other through all those years of school. These people became life-long friends and confidants whether we are able to see each other now or not due to the changes our lives took on as adults. I feel and I hope that if we see each other tomorrow we could sit down and it would be like 1988 all over again.

ॐ I liked that I had friends. I liked the structure.

Public School Disadvantages

ॐ Some of the things I didn't like were always being on my guard to fend off being verbally assaulted by my peers. There was never much physical fighting, although I did get into my first fight in school, which I lost.

ॐ I didn't feel like I was challenged at the school I went to at all. I was bored. I was finishing the work before everyone else. I left campus because I knew the stuff already. Why stay there to learn it again? That was an issue.

ৰ I hated all the homework. To me it was like culture shock, having so much homework every day.

ৰ Definitely dealing with peers and being accepted - to be viewed as cool - was really difficult. I think I worked harder and harder towards that, to be able to gain acceptance through my clothes and through my speech as I started seventh and eighth grade. I had a degree of popularity that I didn't have when I was in fifth and sixth grade. I worked towards that and it certainly changed my behavior for the worse in terms of wanting to fit in.   Other challenges were definitely being around girls, even at that young age of 12 and 13. I was very much noticing girls and other guys were noticing girls. In public school, in fifth grade, kids were having sex. Ten-year old kids were having sex! So seeing all this for the first time was like, "Oh my God, I want some of that too. I want to be a part of that. I want to be a part of the latest new headline that's going on in school." Those were some of the biggest challenges. Luckily,

I never had any challenges related to my safety or anything like that. That was never really an issue. I knew that there were some certain groups of kids that belonged to certain crews that would come at each other after school. The neighborhood that I lived in was kind of close to where some of those guys lived, but I didn't live on that block or directly in that neighborhood.

℘ I had a horrible experience in grammar school. I was the only *Muslimah* in my school (besides one other girl who went there half of the school year and did not cover). The children teased me mercilessly. The kids that went there were just not that accepting of other kids that were different.

℘ There were some students who were very emotionally cruel in school. Due to whatever emotional trauma or neglect they were suffering from, they insisted on verbally torturing me on a daily basis. I was not only the only *Hijabi* in the school, but I was born with a deformity with my hands, which caused all but three of my fingers on both hands to be malformed. These two differences in my appearance often gave students, who were ill-equipped to deal with diversity, rounds and rounds of ammunition for their one-sided "ribb'n sessions." As a child growing up in a Muslim home with two parents in a working-class family, I was not used to these antics and it often sent me into emotional confusion and big *Du'a* sessions with Allah (SWT) for strength and protection. Teachers can only hear and see so much, and in this society, if you tell an adult someone hurt you emotionally or physically, that only makes your social network smaller. So, early on I learned the power of *Du'a*, *Alhamdulillah.*

℘ The bad stuff about public school were the restrictions of the structure and curriculum, the exposure to too many people who have a bad influence, and feeling like an oddball. I was the only *Hijabi* in the school and was new to the public school system. It was very hard relating to other people and feeling like I belonged. I shied away from extracurricular activities, although that probably would've helped a bit.

Can You Stay on Your Deen in Public School?

ഇ Besides the fashion, there was the music. When I started going to public school is when I started listening to *Haram* music. My parents didn't take a really hard stance on music because I'm not sure they 100% understood what was *Halal* and *Haram* music. Obviously, they thought that whatever gangster rap and music with cursing, talking about "f" this, you know, they didn't think that was good for their kids, but at the same time, I don't think that they felt the music of their time, which was a little bit cleaner but was still played in institutions of sin and corruption, was a problem. They didn't think the Four Tops or Temptations were *Haram*, although there were definitely issues they sang about that were. Well, if you're going to be straight and narrow on the music issue with your kids, then you shouldn't listen to similar music from your generation. You can't say it's just party music from an earlier time when it's the same as LL Cool J. If there are exceptions to the music, you have to be clear on which music is *Halal* and why it is an exception. Anyway, the music shapes your thoughts, what's on your mind and your feelings. It affects everything and that definitely moved a lot of Islamic consciousness out of my mind. I think as far as basic fulfillment of *Wajib* acts, I don't think I ever lost that. I always prayed outwardly, but my thoughts were hard to control to maintain that kind of concentration while praying and in between praying. There definitely were certain types of sins that I think I participated in, like wanting to have a girlfriend. I flirted with girls, chatted on the phone, and listened to Haram music and ate Haram meat in the cafeteria. It definitely was hard because I was the only Muslim around.

ෑ *Alhamdulillah,* I was not tempted to do *Haram* things. I think it was only because of the Islamic teachings and identity we kept at home. I think mom staying home with us and being so strong in her *Deen* did it.

ෑ I was not tempted to do any of the

things I saw other kids doing because there were just things that were not allowed in my house. I knew better than to ever contemplate any of the things that they were saying, thinking and doing. It was just like, "Uhhh, no." It was kind of an awed fascination, like watching a train wreck and you can't look the other way. You remember your parents and know that you'll hurt your parents if you did what you knew was wrong. This was when I was about 7 or 8 years old.

ဆ It's kind of difficult. You do have that peer pressure. I do remember a few peers that I talked to… one girl in particular, who used to always ask, "Why are you wearing that thing? Just take it off!" But most of my friends and everybody that I had contact with, most of the time were really nice. Throughout high school, I didn't really have that many problems with peer pressure. I actually was more grounded than I am now. It was in college that I got lulled away from practicing.

ဆ When I went to my friends' house I had to explain that I don't eat pork, I have to pray, no, I can't wear those jeans, shorts or tank tops. It was weird but I was fortunate enough that none of my non-Muslim friends made fun of me. Not to say that I was the perfect Muslim either. There were some things that I did, even if they didn't encourage it. I was being a typical 12 or 13 year old. They wouldn't purposely tempt me, but because I was around them there was more opportunity to do stuff I should not have been doing. Those were my own decisions; there was nothing that they did specifically.

ɞ I ended up completely rebelling against wearing my *Hijab* and covering properly. I always wanted to be like everyone else. I wanted to fit in. I wanted to have friends. After experiencing all the foolishness that came along with that, I ended up coming back around and practicing Islam properly, *Alhamdulillah*. I always had Islam in my heart and never stopped believing in Allah.

ɞ A challenge I faced was being the only *Hijabi* at my school. No one understood that I wore it to please my

Lord and not because I was baldheaded. Before my parents became advocates for me, which didn't take long, I was subjected to many coloring pages of Santa and Thanksgiving Indian and pilgrim scenes, as well as eating lots of Valentine candy and Halloween candy, and learning countless Christmas carols, even in Spanish. Pledging allegiance to a red, white, and blue piece of fabric that has no ability to help itself or me, and having nowhere to offer *Salah* were other issues. And the cafeteria was torture during Ramadan. *Alhamdulillah*, my parents learned while I was still young, maybe by third grade, that they had to write the school often and even show their faces in order to be sure my rights as a Muslim were being met.

Advice to Parents

ഇ My advice would be to approach it creatively. I think homeschooling is not about taking the classroom learning environment and simply transferring it to your home. That's not what homeschooling is. Certainly, we had a component of our day in which we were copying off the blackboard or using a workbook to do all the math times tables. But that wasn't more than two hours. The rest of our schooling was composed of natural, project-based learning experiences where you build something or make something hands-on. The thing is, of course, this makes it harder on the parents. It's more work for the teacher. But all of the latest research in the educational field is saying that so much of the regular sit-and-learn philosophy of this country is just not teaching kids nor helping them obtain information.

ഔ Teaching kids to be able to answer a multiple-choice test does not really help them learn or understand the material. It's all about project-based learning. I'd also say make sure you have a good, dedicated space to homeschool. The environment can really help, even if it's not much. Psychologically, children are able to switch molds when they step into that space and say, "OK, this is the time to sit down and learn and do work." Both parents must get involved in some kind of way. Obviously, we spend more time with our mother than our father, but when my father was around, there were opportunities to learn whatever he was doing. A parent should take the time to teach their child something that they are trying to do. It takes more work trying to teach someone something while also trying to do it. It will take twice as long, but in the long run it's going to benefit your child.

∞ Make sure there is a sense of community with lots of resourceful people and a broad array of activities.

∞ I would look into the programs that are available in your area. Do as much research as you can about other groups that you can get involved in so that your kids are not too sheltered. With me, it turned out that one of my children had some learning disabilities. If you notice some signs that your child has some issues, find out about testing them.

∞ Pay attention to your kids as far as the different things they express that they want to experience. Pay attention to them because they know how they feel and they know what they're lacking in. A kid can become really anti-social and socially awkward if they only stay at home with mom every day. Look around, there are homeschooling groups to meet up with. Try to keep your child as active as possible and not just focused on the academics. Take that extra step to socialize them as well. It's important.

෨ The best advice I could give if you send your kids to public school is to send them there with another good Muslim companion so that they have each other. I think sending a child to public school where they will be by themselves is suicide. At least that was my experience. You always hear about exceptions. Some children are very, very, strong and very, very independent and can resist the outside pressures. They can articulate themselves, and have a degree of confidence in their Islam and their beliefs, but I don't think, typically, that most children are able to get that until they are at least like 10 or 11 or 12 years old, depending on the child.

෨ If you could find another pious

Muslim companion, not just from any Muslim family but from a Muslim family who actually practices, actually trying to improve themselves, that makes a world of difference. We all commit sins and we all have shortcomings, but there's a difference between people who are trying to be religious and improve themselves, and people who just feel that Islam is "whatever" and are not trying to get better. Having a really weak Muslim friend can be worse for a child than not having any Muslim friends at all. Something we all have to infuse in our children, really early, is to go to the source. Children will see hypocrisy. We tell them they can't listen to this or can't do that, but their Muslim friend does it! And if they're my friend, why can't I? What's so bad about it? They begin to question. It just makes your job harder than if, say, they had good Christian friends. At least you could say, "Yeah, they don't do this because they're Christians." Children naturally, at some point, are going to exert a degree of their independence, separate from you, and make their own decisions instead of letting their parents make all the decisions for them. This is natural and this is healthy, but you don't want them to start rebelling against your version of Islam and start following their friends' weaker version of Islam. Your child may think that what they're doing is Islamic as opposed to recognizing that it's at least wrong, and they should be trying to correct these weak Muslims. I'm relating this to my own experience. I knew that when I was going out and going to parties and talking to girls, I knew this was not cool with Islam but I did it because I wanted to. I thought, "Oh, it's not that big a deal." It's not like I ever thought this was *Halal* or good in the eyes of God. I knew it wasn't. But I can see how some Muslims can rationalize anything. The worst thing that could happen is if someone starts doing things that are inappropriate, but they're with friends that have convinced them that this is Islam and is ok. That's horrible. Siblings can be good peers too. Raise them to depend on and love each other.

❧ I went to college with this very religious girl who was also homeschooled. She was Christian. I'm not sure what type. When she got to college, she just went wild. You see these scenarios all the time and it's a shock. At a certain point, at a certain age, children are going to make their own decisions. I've seen it on both extremes, from letting kids do whatever they want, to over-sheltering them from everything. So, I would say communicating with your kids is really important. Talk constantly in terms of what's right and what's wrong and why. Make sure they understand.

დ Oftentimes, when you have a family, you talk about spending family time together with the parents and all the kids. I think this is extremely important and all families should do this. I know I really benefited a lot from it. When each parent takes a little bit of time and does something with just one of the children at a time, a stronger bond is created. They'll see they are getting individual attention, which is very important, especially in large families. I remember things were so different when it was just me and my mom as opposed to my mom, my sisters and me. It's totally different. The conversations were different because it was no longer one-on-one. The whole social dynamic changed. I think we as parents give the best of ourselves to our children when we're only focusing on one child. That's not always possible, but it's something that you can try to do every now and then. Of course, you have to rotate and take turns, but it doesn't need to be a lot of time, just be consistent. Find a day, an afternoon, a few hours with just you and one kid. When you have aunts and uncles that can do the same, that's good too.

෨ **Be okay with the fact that your kids are going to make mistakes**. Don't be so stern that your kid is not going to want to come to you and tell you anything. I got to a point in my life where I was doing this or that, not out of fear or loyalty to Allah, but out of fear of my dad. And that's where a lot of my conflict with Islam started happening. Later on, when I was 17 or 18, I started questioning a lot of stuff and had a lot of squabbles with my parents.

෨ I was scared to come to my parents for anything. Definitely don't let a wall develop between you and your kids because it's going to take forever to come back down. You have to willingly have that open dialogue and be prepared to hear what you may not want to hear.

℘ This may sound really wild, or old fashioned, or extremely radical, but I think the Prophet's (PBUH) advice to marry young and stay married is an important thing to consider bringing back. At least consider it. I'm sure some young adults would not mind. I know it would've been something that would've helped me. The biggest thing about growing up is maturing sexually. It takes over your mind - and when you go to public school where girls are showing breasts and legs and are all made-up to entice, there are going to be problems. There is no way around it. The boys go crazy and the girls who dress that way are doing it for the attention of the boys! It's playing with a fire that God has instilled in mankind and one that can only be regulated by His laws. There no such thing as adolescence in Islam. You're either a child or an adult and the physical signs of adulthood are clear. This society likes to keep people immature and wary of marriage. It wants us to play too much for too long and play with things that are not to be played with: relationships and sex. If, say, young adults who are fourteen, fifteen, or sixteen are allowed to get married and still live at home with one or the other parents, it would solve almost ALL the issues we find in high school. They would mature quickly and have their spouse. They can wait to have children. My mother used to tell me this was common just two generations ago and not that rare here in America. Of course, you can't do this all of a sudden. The children have to be raised to expect and grow towards young marriage - and you need to have a lot of contacts with young boys and girls that they can meet and talk to for that purpose, and the families get to know each other - and be given responsibilities and training along those lines. One of the problems with kids being so immature is that they are continually told they are! Something like this won't be able to happen overnight - it will take time, but I think after all this time of kids committing huge sins due to an environment that encourages these sins; the only way to counter them is with the tried and true advice of Prophet Muhammad (PBUH).

&) I think that, if you send your child to public school, it's a gamble. You never know for sure what they will end up doing. Some kids can handle it. They are not tempted to do anything outside the perimeters of Islam. They remember everything you say and remain unscathed by peer pressure and all the goings-on around them. I was not like that at all. I wanted a boyfriend. I wanted to party and to wear cool clothes. Eventually, I ended up drinking alcohol and smoking weed as well. Yeah, I was a Muslim parent's worst nightmare! A child may not end up doing all that, but you never know how far they will go. Or, they may maintain their *Deen* until they go off to college and then let loose.

&) I definitely recommend homeschooling if you can. Make *Du'a* because homeschooling does not guarantee that your child will be a *Mu'min* either. I believe it gives you a better chance, but there are no guarantees. Prophet Nuh's (AS) son became a *Kafir* and he was the son of a Prophet! If you can't homeschool, make *Du'a*. That had to be what saved me 'cause I was way out there.

  My advice to parents who send their children to public school is to be involved. YOU are your child's guidance counselor and advocate! Let their school know who you are, who your child is, and that you all are practicing, unapologetic Muslims. Don't think allowing your child the public school experience will not influence their *Deen* because it will. If you aren't involved, the negative influences will outweigh your home lifestyle.

  Make sure to keep an open dialogue with your child and share your own experiences in school. Keep a steady Islamic environment with Islamic teachings and relate them to their experiences. Encourage your children to ask questions.

  One thing I want to mention is the mixing of the sexes at public school.

Don't think there is no sexual harassment within the schools amongst children (starting even earlier than junior high school nowadays). It's there and it's rampant due to the oversexed TV shows, movies, videos and music. Children are being exposed to sex much earlier and their curiosity is causing them to explore. May Allah protect our children who are in public schools, and make it easier on us who don't have the option to homeschool or send our precious ones to a *Madrassa... Ameen.*

ဆ Fight for your child's right to exercise his/her religion. Arrange for them to be able to make *Salah* in a separate room at *Salah* time. See if they can get out of school early on Fridays for *Jumuah*. Let the teacher know that we do not pledge allegiance to the flag, and so on.

ဆ My advice is that, by high school, DO NOT put your children in public school. Take them out by the time they reach "the hormone stage," and for some children, that's by the seventh or eighth grade. It's just too dangerous. They are old enough to take care of themselves at home if need be, or stay with another family with an adult during the day if you work. They can do independent study, take the GED, work, start their own business, help with your home business (if you have one), stay at the library reading and researching, do "real" education in the real world with the community, etc. Travel - maybe in some kind of exchange program - is ideal at this time. Volunteering, especially serving people in dire situations is humbling and eye-opening. If you have an active Islamic community, they can come up with ideas to implement to help in that capacity. I'm not saying they can't socialize or meet or "be" with other young adults, but high schools are a lot "freer" than the younger grades and all kinds of things happen, out in the open, boldly and with purpose. Our purpose as Muslims is diametrically opposed to most of what is acceptable there. Look at public school as a dangerous place and deal with it accordingly.

No matter what you choose - homeschool or public school - there is always a chance that your child may stray off the path of Islam. The better you and your family practice Islam, and the more consistent you teach Islam to your children while maintaining a good relationship with them, the better chance they will stay on *Sirat al-Mustaqeem*. As always, lots and lots of *Du'a* are needed.

But Allah is the best to take care (of him), and He is the Most Merciful of those who show mercy!
                                              (Quran 12:64)

Glory to Thee! Our (tie) is with Thee - as Protector - not with them.
                                              (Quran 34:41)

Allah sufficeth me: there is no God but He: On Him is my trust. He is the Lord of the Throne (of Glory) Supreme!"
                                              (Quran 9:129)

Chapter 9: Sending Your Child to Public School

When done correctly, there are countless benefits in teaching your child at home. I urge all parents to at least give it a try before writing it off as being too difficult a task to pursue. That being said, it is not always possible for a family to make that choice. If, for whatever reason, you choose to send your child to public school, there are many actions that you can take to ensure that your children will have the best experience possible while not losing their Islamic identity, *Insha'Allah.*

  ⅎ The first thing that you have to do is keep your door and ears open. Talk to your child. Find out what's going on with him or her. Don't make it so that you don't know about their school life. Get involved. Don't be ashamed to participate. Let the kids see you. Let them see that you're a supportive mom or dad. I chat with the teachers. I'm letting them know, "Hey, this is my child and I'm here if there's a problem. Do not hesitate to call me, I will be right here." This gives the kids a sense of security knowing their parents are going to stop whatever they're doing to come to school if need be.

℘ You don't have to be the PTA president, but join the PTA and be active. Notice if your child is coming home with torn clothing or if something new is going on. Boys can blend in ok, but it is really hard for girls, especially when they wear the *Khimar* all the way down below their knees. Now, that's pretty hard. Maybe we can just let the *Khimar* come down to the breast level. They can be different but not "so" different.

℘ Volunteer at your child's school as much as possible. If you can volunteer to be an aid or help with field trips, do so! This may be difficult if you are working, but get involved with the PTA and do what you can after work. Make sure you talk to the teachers as much as possible. Develop a good relationship with your child and ask him how his day has gone, every day. Learn to read between the lines and watch for mood swings. Find out what's wrong, if anything.

ഔ Be reasonable and realistic. If you choose public school, realize you have to make a DECISION to be PURPOSEFUL in educating your child about the *Deen* and forming their character. Don't let the school day end until some form of Islamic character lessons has been incorporated.

ഔ Work on your children day and night. Tell them the sayings of the Rasool (PBUH) and his household as well as verses from the Quran as part of your normal daily conversation. This way they can absorb it and develop an Islamic mindset and frame of reference.

ഔ Don't be lazy. This is your child. Research the school. Be at the school every day. From my experience, teachers care about the students that they think are cared for. If they think that this person's family loves this child they will keep an eye out for that child. If they see little Muhammad over there with a group of kids he's not supposed to be hanging out with, maybe they might say something to him about it. I remember teachers telling me, "You know your mama raised you better than that," or "You know you shouldn't be doing that." At least develop a rapport with the teachers so they will say something to you. If they feel like a child's parents are not involved, hasn't called, emailed or even met them, that's how she's going to treat your kid. It's really nothing personal; they have nearly thirty other children to contend with. The squeaky wheel gets the attention!

෬ Talk to your child about being proud of who he or she is and not to feel ashamed. Explain to them that others will respect them if they stand up for what they believe in. Encourage them to be leaders and not followers, to pick and choose their friends well and to set high standards for those they choose as friends. They need to understand that they don't have to apologize for being different or try to change to be like everyone else. If they go in there with their head up and with a strong sense of self, representing Islam, they will be alright, *Insha'Allah.*

෬ For older kids, don't preach - DIALOGUE! Talk to your kids about what they think the important issues of the day are and how they relate to the *Deen.* Talk to them about sex, dating and drugs. Be "real." Listen to what they are trying to say to you and appreciate the forces pulling at them from all sides. Don't just tell them, "Don't do that because Allah (SWT) says so." Give them strategies to get out of tough spots and give them lessons from your real life about how these things end up. Role-play at home.

ဢ Don't just talk about charity, show them. Do a service project as a family. Sew *Eid* outfits together. It's great if they can learn Quranic *Ayahs* and *Hadith* that address these things. If they are too young to understand, it's still important to get them used to doing good deeds for the sake of Allah (SWT) from an early age.

ဢ Give them opportunities to make Muslim friends. Get them involved in Muslim youth groups.

ဢ DON'T be:
• Pushy
• Judgmental

- The type of parents who constantly scream about fire and brimstone
- A poor listener
- Unavailable or dismissive
- The type of parent who uses Islam as a punishment
- Afraid to apologize and admit when you were wrong
- Let your temper get the best of you

ॐ For younger kids, the trick is routine. Start as soon as they are born. Remember, you're also training yourself how to be a good parent and teacher so get a head start. They "hear" everything we do, so it's important that we try to put forth a good and consistent example. Be creative! Islam is not supposed to be dry and painful. I teach new *Surahs* by reciting them at bedtime like a bedtime prayer. It's part of our routine. We put up *Ramadan* lights and make a *Ramadan* wall with pictures and cut-out letters every year. I send my daughter to school with cupcakes on the Islamic New Year and the *Eids.* Mixed in with her schoolbooks are storybook versions of the lives of the Prophets (AS). And sometimes I "Islamicize" regular stories while I tell them. In this way, Islam is simply part of my daughter's everyday life.

ဢ My grammar school was walking distance from our house. It took us about 15 minutes to walk there and all along the way my mother gave me religious instruction. She taught me the Arabic alphabet and various *Surahs* and expounded upon various Islamic topics. I think this is a very good time to drop a few pearls of Islamic wisdom on your child, at the beginning of the day, so that's what they carry with them throughout the rest of the day. I learned a lot during those brief morning walks to school and I'm sure your child will too.

ဢ For all parents: get involved in your kids' school. Go on field trips, become a real partner in the learning process with the teacher. Nobody knows how your child learns better than you. Give your kids' teachers a clue. Ask if you can do things at home to supplement what is happening in the classroom. Don't be afraid to suggest and provide supplemental classroom materials like articles on historical events and worksheets. The more of a presence you have as a good parent the less likely it is that teachers will ignore, stereotype or mistreat your child. Also, you'll be more aware when "negative school influences" begin to take root in your child and you can, *Insha'Allah,* nip it in the bud.

৪০ Remember, we are fighting against a world that is in chaos, so pray for your children all the time. I make *Du'a* with and for my little one every morning while we wait for the school bus. Once again, it's a routine that teaches her to include Islam in every part of her life. We also need the wisdom and protection that only Allah (SWT) can provide for our little ones.

৪০ Hug and kiss your kids. I know it seems like it isn't related to education or Islam, but physical affection is so important to how kids feel about themselves and you and EVERYTHING you are trying to teach them. DADS should especially hug their kids, even the teens, especially the teenage girls. I know that dads tend to back off when girls hit puberty, but that's when she needs you more than ever. If you pull away and become distant, she will react, even if she isn't really sure what she's reacting to. Hug them, kiss them, hold their hand, tell them you love them and they will see you and the values you represent in a more positive light.

ဆ As your child gets older, find out what kind of independent studies are available. I believe 13 is the age where you can legally keep your child at home alone, if need be, although most of the time they can be at another Muslim family's home doing their work independently, maybe helping out the mom there - especially if she homeschools.

ဆ At a certain point, going to public school can become a real social nightmare. Try as you might to be involved, those five to eight hours in a secular environment with peers, who they come to like and respect, will take its toll on your child's behavior and outlook. At this point (actually before, if you can), look seriously into finding another homeschooling family that is willing to let your child do independent study in their home, and/or who can help teach them. Bargain for a proper tuition amount that's fair or a trade, like you keeping their children on the weekends or for x-amount of hours when they need it. Make sure you inundate your child with Islamic activities, Islamic home study, and weekend school. Be real about what they are seeing and experiencing in school and discuss it through an Islamic framework. Depending on the child, sometimes you just have to lay down the law and infuse the fear of disobeying and angering you and your husband and God. Being too nice and understanding for things and situations children KNOW better than to get involved with or do - repeatedly - is cause for alarm and immediate attention and change. Seek Allah's help and He will help you figure out what to do to fix it.

Most importantly, remember the power of prayer. We should pray to Allah (SWT) first to show us the best action to take. Then we must pray to Him to bless us with the very best outcome. Whatever we do, we have to remember that we need to back up all our actions with sincere *Du'a* to Allah (SWT). Allah (SWT) will answer our *Du'as*. As He says in the Holy Quran:

And when My servants ask you concerning Me, then surely I am very near; I answer the prayer of the supplicant when he calls on Me, so they should answer My call and believe in Me that they may walk in the right way.

(Quran 2:186)

...surely Thou art the Hearer of prayer.

(Quran 3:38)

Say: My Lord has enjoined justice, and set upright your faces at every time of prayer and call on Him, being sincere to Him in obedience."

(Quran 7:29)

...Most surely my Lord is the Hearer of prayer....

(Quran 14:39)

Famous and Homeschooled

Though homeschooling has become more popular in the United States and abroad in recent years, it is not a new concept. Many famous people were homeschooled at some point in their lives, including but not limited to presidents, authors, inventors, artists, and scientists. This lends credibility to the fact that homeschoolers can grow up to be sociable and successful contributors to society. I've included below a list of eleven famous people who were homeschooled:

ɢ **Tennis Pros Venus and Serena Williams** were homeschooled by their father, who taught them from middle school to high school. As part of their education, they spoke in inner-city schools and put on tennis clinics for disadvantaged youth.

ɢ **Booker T. Washington** was a teacher, author, and founder of the Tuskegee Institute. He had no formal education as a young boy. He was unable to attend school because he had to work to help support his family. He taught himself the alphabet and studied as much as he could after work. Later on, he attended college at Hampton Institute, and upon graduating, attended Wayland Seminary so that he could become a teacher.

ๆ **Thomas Edison**, the inventor of the phonograph and the light bulb, originally attended a traditional school. He often daydreamed and was quite bored in class. Consequently, his teacher thought that he was "dull" and told his mother that he was "unteachable." Mrs. Edison removed him from the school and taught him herself.

ๆ **Phyllis Wheatley**, the famous poet, was taught by her master's 18 year old daughter, Mary. By the time she was 12 years old, Phyllis had developed an amazing literary ability and was allowed more time to study. She began to write poetry at the age of 13. She never attended a formal school.

ๆ **Christopher Paolini** self-published the book, *Eragon,* when he was 19 years old. He was homeschooled for the majority of his life and graduated high school at the age of 15. Upon graduation, Christopher began writing *Eragon*, which ultimately ended up grossing $249 million worldwide due to his brilliant marketing strategy.

ๆ **Pierre Curie** was a French physicist, a pioneer in crystal-lography, magnetism, piezoelectricity and radioactivity, and a Nobel laureate. Pierre was educated at home by his father.

ๆ **Clara Barton** was an American pioneer who was schooled at home. She became a teacher, nurse, and humanitarian and was the founder of the American Red Cross.

ဢ **Florence Nightingale** received a classical education from her father. She became a nurse, writer and statistician. She opened the first secular nursing school in the world at St. Thomas' Hospital in 1860, which laid the foundation for professional nursing.

ဢ **Blaise Pascal,** a French inventor, writer, and mathematician, was educated by his father at home. He invented the mechanical calculator.

ဢ **Benjamin Franklin** helped create the American system of government. He was also an inventor, scientist, author, and printer. Benjamin attended school for only two years, continuing his education through avid reading.

Homeschooled children can definitely do well in college, but many opt not to. Contrary to popular belief, a person does not have to attend college in order to have a successful life. Many parents despair at the thought of their children not going to college. They believe the only way to achieve success in life is to acquire a college degree. This is obviously not true. Many successful men and women either dropped out after a few semesters or never went at all. Likewise, there are many people with college degrees who can't find decent jobs.

Successful Without College

෧ **Henry Ford** never graduated from high school, but he founded the Ford Motor Company, the first and largest automobile manufacturing company at the time. He is the sponsor of the development of the assembly line technique of mass production, which revolutionized transportation and American industry.

෧ **Bill Gates** dropped out of college after two years to form a partnership with classmate Paul Allen. They formed the billion-dollar company known as Microsoft. According to Forbes magazine, Bill Gates' net worth was $54 billion in 2010.

෧ **Milton Hershey**, philanthropist and entrepreneur, dropped out of school at the age of 13 due to his family's constant moving. After a four-year apprenticeship and a few failed attempts, he eventually founded the well-known candy company, the Hershey Chocolate Corporation.

෧ **Rachael Ray** has never had any formal training in culinary arts despite the fact that she is a well-known name in the food industry. She is a very successful American television personality, celebrity chef and author. Ray says that her Sicilian maternal grandfather, Emmanuel Scuderi, as well as her Cajun ancestry, serves as a strong influence on her cooking.

ℋ **Debbi Fields** started Mrs. Fields Chocolate Chippery at the age of 20. She was a young housewife with no college degree and no prior business experience. Nevertheless, Mrs. Fields became the single most successful cookie company owner in America.

ℋ **Wolfgang Puck is** a famous Austrian-American celebrity chef, restaurateur, and businessman. He learned cooking from his mother and by working in many fine restaurants in France and the United States.

ℋ **Dave Thomas** the founder and chief executive officer of Wendy's Old Fashioned Hamburgers did not finish high school.

ℋ **Steve Jobs** is an American business tycoon and inventor. He is the co-founder and chief executive officer of Apple. He dropped out of college after only one semester, but continued auditing classes at Reed College. Forbes magazine estimated his net wealth at $6.1 billion in 2010, making him the 42nd wealthiest person in America.

ℋ **David Karp** is the founder and CEO of the popular short-form blogging platform, Tumblr. At age 15, he stopped attending public school and was homeschooled. He did not attend college.

ℋ **Billy Joe (Red) McCombs** is the billionaire founder of the Red McCombs Automotive Group, the Clear Channel media empire, and is a real estate investor. Billy dropped out of law school to sell cars in 1950. He owned his first automobile dealership by the age of 25.

Glossary of Homeschool Terms

Blog: A word that blends the terms web and log. It is an interactive website or part of a website which provides commentary or news on a particular subject. They are usually run by an individual who posts commentary, graphics, videos, and/or pictures on a chosen topic. Blogs are an excellent way to learn more about homeschooling.

UAE
K12, Timberdoodle, Ad Duha

Boxed Curriculum: Also known as School-In-A-Box, it refers to a complete package of curriculum that includes all the materials a student needs for his or her particular grade level, including tests, workbooks, textbooks, activity suggestions and a teacher's manual. This program is ideal for those who prefer a traditional, more structured approach to homeschooling.

Burnout: A term used to describe when a parent or child has become exhausted from the process of homeschooling.

Calvert School: The oldest distance-learning program for children in the United States. Calvert offers a complete homeschooling program for children in grades pre-K through 8. Parents purchase the curriculum package for their child's grade level. These packages come complete with textbooks,

233

workbooks, and all of the materials needed to complete the course of study. This program is ideal for those who prefer a traditional, structured approach to homeschooling. *Note: Not all correspondence schools offer accredited diplomas. If this is important to you, check with each individual school to find out if they are accredited in your state.

Charter Schools: Non-traditional public schools that offer more flexibility to teachers and students. These schools are not subject to some of the rules, regulations, and statutes that apply to regular public schools. Some offer "home study programs" wherein the student is assigned an "education facilitator" who meets with parents and students once a month to discuss progress, collect work samples, and attendance sheets. Individual charter school programs may provide educational credits to be used for the purchase of an educational curriculum and or any class or outside vendored lessons the child wants to take.

living books => Atmosphere, discipline, life

Charlotte Mason Education: Named after the 19th century educator, Miss Charlotte Mason, who said that children learned best by observation and narration. Her method encourages students to observe and create. The goal of Mason education is to provide the child with a lifelong love and quest for knowledge, and the skills to succeed in that quest.

CHSPE (California High School Proficiency Exam): An exam that a student can take before official graduation. It is equivalent to a high school diploma in California. In order to take this exam, the student must be at least 16 years old or have completed at least one academic year of the 10th grade.

Trivium

Classical Education: Also called trivium-based education, it is a history-based approach to education that divides education into three stages: grammar in early elementary school, logic in middle school, and rhetoric in high school. *Note: If you are interested in this teaching style, read the book *"The Well-Trained Mind"* by Jessie Wise and Susan Wise Bauer.

Core Subjects: Refers to the main subject matter a child is required to learn. According to "The No Child Left Behind Act of 2001," the "core academic subjects" are:

English   Reading or Language Arts
Mathematics   Science
Foreign Languages   Civics and Government
Economics   Arts
History   Geography

Cooperative (Co-Op): Refers to a cooperative of families who homeschool their children together. There is an opportunity for more socialization amongst the children. They may take classes together or go on field trips. Parents teach the subjects that they are more specialized in.

Cover School: Also known as an umbrella school, this is a school that enrolls homeschooling children or families and offers services supportive of home education.

Curriculum: Refers to any materials used to teach subjects including but not limited to workbooks, textbooks, worksheets, software, activities, and so on.

Cyber Schools: Also known as virtual schools, these schools can be attended via the Internet. A student takes all or most of the required courses for a degree, diploma or certificate online. Some are free and some charge a fee.

Diagnostic Testing: These types of tests measure a child's strengths and weaknesses. An initial test determines whether further testing is required to determine if a child may have a learning disability or other special needs. You can secure diagnostic tests from different curriculum providers and online sources. If you are with a homeschooling program, you may be able to access the test for free.

Eclectic Approach: A method of teaching that does not rely on any one approach but rather utilizes the teaching method and style that works best for the individual child.

GED: This is an abbreviation for the General Equivalency Diploma. Homeschoolers can take the GED test to prove that they are proficient in high school academic skills. Upon completing and passing the test, students receive a certificate similar to a diploma and can usually go on to community college for further education.

Holt, John: is a pioneer of the modern homeschool and un-school movement. Holt believed that, given the opportunity, children will learn naturally. The idea is to give them the freedom to follow their own interests with access to a rich assortment of resources. He founded the "Growing Without Schooling" movement that publishes the Growing Without Schooling magazine and has authored a number of books including the homeschool classic, *"Teach Your Own."*

Home Education Magazine: This is the oldest homeschooling magazine and is available nationwide.

Homeschool Support Group: A group of homeschooling families that come together periodically to share information, encouragement and to provide cooperative educational and social activities for the children. Activities vary from group to group. Some may have play-days, organized classes, or field trips. Some are religion-specific and some are all-inclusive. Check online to find a local homeschool support group in your area.

IEP: stands for Individual Educational Plan. This is an individualized plan used by public schools to write, evaluate, diagnose and set goals and teaching strategies for primarily disabled students. Any child who receives special education and related services must have an IEP.

Lapbook: This is basically a manila file folder, refolded, creased and turned into a learning scrapbook. A lapbook may contain facts, diagrams, illustrations, etc., related to the subject. It can be simple, with just a picture and definition. Or it can be complex with pockets, flaps, pop-ups, origami folds and more.

Learning Methods: Also known as "learning styles," this phrase refers to the different ways children and adults naturally learn best. Most people are a combination of more than one learning style, but usually one style is dominant over another. Knowing your child's learning style, and teaching according to that style, will engage him on that level and will enable your child to better retain the material. The number of learning styles can vary in number, but the three main styles are:

1. Auditory (learning by hearing)
2. Visual (learning by seeing)
3. Kinesthetic (learning by doing)

Math Manipulatives: Hands-on educational tools that help students build concrete models of abstract math concepts so they can better understand them. Manipulatives help students connect math terminology and symbols in a practical way. Manipulatives include blocks, Cuisenaire rods, color tiles, popsicle sticks, counters, spinners, beans, pebbles, interlocking cubes, and number lines, etc.

 Montessori Education: Founded by Dr. Maria Montessori, who specialized in child development, this schooling method follows the natural emotional, physical and mental development of children. The child is allowed to progress at his or her own pace, and according to their own individual capabilities, through practical play. The teacher observes while the child freely uses the various self-teaching materials. The teacher steps in only if needed, mainly to resolve any misbehavior issues, or to show the child how to use something.

Notebooking: A popular educational method which entails journaling or keeping track of homeschool studies and educational experiences in a notebook or three-ring binder. Students take notes or write down their thoughts on what they are learning. They may also add pages with photos or illustrations.

Online Support Groups: Homeschooling parents who offer each other support through e-mail lists or forum message boards on the Internet. They lack face-to-face contact, but are especially valuable for those who don't know other homeschoolers, and for those who are on a tight schedule and don't want to get involved in a busy local group.

Phonics: A reading method used to learn how to read and write English. Phonics familiarizes students with the various English sounds and the letters they correspond to. Once they have mastered the main sounds, they can then read many English words.

Portfolio: A record of a homeschool student's educational career, which includes reading and attendance logs, assignments, writing samples, pictures of projects, field trips, and awards, certificates of completion and more.

Private School Affidavit: Formerly known as an R-4 form, this form is used by homeschoolers in California to notify the state that they have established a private school. If you live in California and plan to instruct your child at home without enrolling them in any type of homeschool, you will need this form to file with the Board of Education.

School at Home: Refers to the method of setting up your home in a way that duplicates the methods and atmosphere of a traditional classroom.

Standardized Test: State or federal tests that are used to evaluate how well a child has learned a subject or grade level when compared to other children in his grade and age group. Some states require homeschoolers to take standardized tests. Studies have shown that homeschoolers consistently outscore government-schooled children. These test results don't necessarily indicate achievement.

Waldorf Schooling: A philosophy of teaching based on using the kinesthetic form of learning, developed by Rudolf Steiner. Waldorf emphasizes the role of the imagination in learning. Subjects are introduced creatively through stories, art, and music.

Glossary of Islamic Terms

<u>Abayah</u>: A long over-garment, essentially a robe-like dress, worn by some Muslim women

<u>Adab</u>: In the context of behavior, refers to prescribed Islamic etiquette: "refinement, good manners, morals, decorum, decency, humaneness."

<u>Adthan</u>: The Islamic way of calling Muslims to the five obligatory prayers. The Adthan is announced daily from the Mosques and in the homes of Muslims. (also spelled Adhan).

<u>Akhirah</u>: The 'hereafter' or life after death

<u>Alhamdulillah</u>: Means "The praise (is) to Allah (God)."

<u>Allah</u>: The Arabic word for the One God.

<u>Ameen</u>: Means "So be it." (also spelled Amin).

<u>Aqeeda</u>: Can mean covenant, agreed upon law, ideology or ideological belief. It can also mean tradition.

<u>Ayah</u>: A verse in the Quran

Ayat al-Kursi: Known as "The Throne of the Quran" verse, it is the 255th verse (Ayah) of the second chapter (Surah), Al-Baqarah. It is one of the most famous verses of the Quran and is widely memorized and displayed in Muslim homes, etc. due to its emphatic description of God's power over the entire universe.

Dawah: Propagation of Islam through word and action, calling the people to follow the commandments of Allah and His Messenger Prophet Muhammad (SAW).

Deen: Is sometimes translated as "religion," but as used in the Quran, it refers to the path along which righteous Muslims travel in order to comply with divine law, or Shari'a, in preparation for facing God's divine judgment.

Dhikr: An Islamic devotional act, typically involving the repetition of the names of God, supplications or formulas taken from Hadith texts and/or verses of the Quran.

Du'a: Supplication, to invoke Allah for whatever one desires.

Dunya: The temporal world and its earthly concerns and possessions, as opposed to the eternal spiritual realm, or the hereafter (Akhirah).

Eid: Festival.

Eid al-Adha: A four-day festival that completes the rites of pilgrimage and takes place on the 10th-13th of the Islamic month, Dhul Hijjah. Eid Al-Adha literally means "the feast of the sacrifice." This feast commemorates Prophet Ibrahim's obedience to Allah by his willingness to sacrifice his only son, Ismail, peace be upon both of them. See: Holy Quran, As-Saffaat (37:100-103).

Fajr: Dawn. It is also the name of the first Islamic prayer during the daytime. It can be prayed at any time between the first light of dawn and just before sunrise.

Fiqh: Islamic jurisprudence

Fisabilillah: Means "In the cause of, or for the sake of Allah."

Hadith: Literally means communication or narration. In the Islamic context it has come to denote the record of what the Prophet (SAW) said, did, or tacitly approved.

Haram: (1) Sin: any act prohibited by Allah that will incur His wrath and punishment. (2) Sanctuary or boundary of any Masjid (mosque), but usually used with regard to the sanctuaries of the Masjid al-Haram in Makkah and Masjid ar-Rasool in Madinah.

Hijab: Refers to both the head covering traditionally worn by Muslim women and modest Muslim dress styles in general.

Hijabi: A female that wears Hijab.

Hilal: Arabic term meaning crescent moon; the very slight crescent moon that is first visible after a new moon. Muslims look for the Hilal when determining the beginning and end of Islamic months.

Ibadah: Three meanings: (1) worship and adoration; (2) obedience and submission; and (3) service and subjection.

Iftar: Breaking of the fast immediately after sunset during Ramadan, the month of fasting.

Insha'Allah: Means "If Allah wills."

Isha: One of the five obligatory daily prayers, performed after the sun has set and the night has well set-in.

Istikharah: A special prayer asking Allah the Almighty to guide one to the right decision and action regarding a particular problem.

Jamat: Community

Jumuah: It is equivalent to the English word, Friday, often called the Muslim "holy day." It also refers to the community congregational prayer at Masjids that take place on Friday afternoons.

Jilbab: The plural of the word Jilaabah referring to any long and loose-fit coat or garment worn by some Muslim women.

Kafir: One who denies or rejects the truth, i.e. who disbelieves in the message of the Prophets.

Khimar: Headscarf.

Kufi: A brimless, short, rounded cap worn by African people and Muslims.

Madrassa: An Islamic School

Maghrib: The fourth obligatory prayer of the day, made at sunset.

Masha'Allah: Means "God has willed it."

Mu'min: A Muslim who is a strong believer in Allah, Prophet Muhammad (SAW) and the Quran. Their faith dictates that they submit without hesitation. A Mu'min is considered more religious than the term, "Muslim."

Muslimah: Female Muslim

Muqaddimah: A book written by the North African historian, Ibn Khaldun in 1377.

Nabi: Prophet of Allah.

Nasheeds: Islamic songs unaccompanied with music.

Nikah: The matrimonial contract in an Islamic marriage.

Nuh: Prophet Noah.

Rasool (Rasul): Messenger from God with divine codes of law. Often used to refer to Prophet Muhammad (SAW) as the Messenger or Ambassador of God who brought the holy book, the Quran. Rasool is higher in rank than Nabi (prophet). Of the 25 Prophets mentioned in Quran, only 5 were also Rasools: Nuh, Ibrahim, Moses, Isa (Jesus) and Muhammad (SAW).

Rasulullah: Messenger of Allah.

Sadaqah: Voluntary charity given at any time.

Sajdah: Prostration. The act of prostration, particularly in the Salah.

Salah: Prayers that Muslims perform daily. There are five daily obligatory prayers (also spelled Salat):

1. *Fajr* (morning prayer); After dawn but before sunrise;

2. *Dhuhr* (early afternoon or noon prayer); early afternoon till late afternoon;

3. *'Asr* (late afternoon prayer) late afternoon prayer till sunset;

4. *Maghrib* (sunset prayer) just after sunset;

5. *Isha* (late evening prayer) late evening till late at night.

Shaytan: Satan

Sirat al-Mustaqeem: The Straight Path (way)

Sunnah: The way of life prescribed for Muslims on the basis of the teachings and practices of Muhammad (SAW) and interpretations of the Quran.

Surah: A chapter of the Quran. Literally means "a form." There are 114 Surahs in the Holy Quran.

Suratul: Another form of the word Surah based upon

grammatical rules in Arabic. The 'tul' is usually added when a name of a particular Surah immediately follows it.

Ta'aleem: Education. Usually refers to a speech or lesson on various religious precepts, philosophy and history of Quran, Hadith and/or Islamic history.

Tarawiyah: Special group prayers done after Isha (night) prayers during Ramadan, the fasting month.

Tarbiya: The process of individuals developing the character and behavior that exemplify Islamic teachings in their daily life.

Tafsir: A commentary, usually referring to the commentary of the Holy Quran.

Tahajjud: A highly recommended but not obligatory Salah performed alone, between midnight and dawn.

Wajib: Obligatory.

Wudhu: Refers to the ablution (washing of hands, face, arms and feet) made before performing the prescribed Prayers (Salah).

Zakat: Giving a percentage of one's surplus wealth in charity to the poor and needy. This is given after the completion of fasting during the holy month of

Ramadan.

<u>Zawj</u>: Spouse (husband or wife), although 'Zawj' is sometimes used to refer to husband, 'zawjah' to wife. In Arabic, it literally means "partner or reproductive half."

Recommended Reading List

If you're a new homeschooler, a seasoned homeschooler, or still undecided, it is important that you read about educating your own as much as you can. The more knowledge you acquire, the more confidence you'll gain in your teaching skills. There is a plethora of reading material available. Just to get you started, below is a very short list of books I have found helpful.

Homeschooling In General

1. *Homeschooling for Success (How Parents Can Create a Superior Education for Their Child)* by Rebecca Kochenderfer & Elizabeth Kanna

2. *Homeschooling at the Speed of Life (Balancing Home, School and Family in the Real World)* by Marilyn Rockett

3. *Developing & Educating the Islamic Child: Islamic Education Manual* by Umm Sulaiman (may be out of print)

4. *The Well Trained Mind: A Guide to Classical Education at Home* by Susan Wise Bauer and Jessie Wise

5. *Balancing Life as a Muslim Mom* by Ponn Sabra

6. *The Busy Mom's Guide to a Happy, Organized Home* by Kathy Peel

Homeschooling Teens

7. *The 7 Habits of Highly Effective Teens* by Sean Covey

8. *Muslim Teens: Today's Worry, Tomorrow's Hope* by Dr. Ekram & Mohamed R. Beshir

9. *Homeschooling The Teen Years: Your Complete Guide to Homeschooling Your 13- to 18-Year Old* by Cafi Cohen

Thematic Teaching through Literature

10. *Five in a Row, Volume 1 (ages 5-8)* by Jane Claire Lambert

11. *Five in a Row for 8-12, Volume 1* by Jane Claire Lambert

12. *Before Five in a Row (ages 2-4)* by Jane Claire Lambert

13. *Homeschooling at the Speed of Life* by Marilyn Rocket